T0147015

MY TEACHING

MY TEACHING

JACQUES LACAN

Translated by David Macey

VERSO

London • New York

This edition first published by Verso 2008
© Verso 2008
Translation © David Macey 2008
First published as *Mon Enseignement*
© Éditions du Seuil 2005
All rights reserved

1 3 5 7 9 10 8 6 4 2

Verso
UK: 6 Meard Street, London W1F 0EG
US: 388 Atlantic Ave, Brooklyn, NY 11217
www.versobooks.com

Verso is the imprint of New Left Books

ISBN-13: 978-1-84467-270-7 (hbk)
ISBN-13: 978-1-84467-271-4 (pbk)

British Library Cataloguing in Publication Data
A catalogue record for this book is available from the British Library

Library of Congress Cataloging-in-Publication Data
A catalog record for this book is available from the Library of Congress

Typeset by Hewer Text UK Ltd, Edinburgh
Printed in the US

CONTENTS

PREFACE

It was 1967, and then 1968, before the month of May. *Écrits* had been published in late 1966. Lacan was invited everywhere to talk about it. He sometimes accepted the invitations and went to various provincial towns.[1]

He found himself faced with audiences who were not familiar with what he called his 'same old story'. He improvised, described his difficulties with his colleagues, and expounded the concepts of psychoanalysis in the most accessible style. He was funny. For example: 'We've always known about the unconscious. But in psycho-analysis, the unconscious is an unconscious that thinks hard. Just a minute, just a minute.'

---

1 He also visited Italy, where he gave three lectures. The text, which was written in advance, is included in *Autres écrits*, Paris: Seuil, 2001, 329–359.

Sometimes it even sounded like a sketch by someone like Pierre Dac, Devos or Bedos:[2]

Psychoanalysts do not say that they know in so many words, but they imply that they do. 'We do know a bit about it, but let's keep quiet about that. Let's keep it between ourselves.' We enter this field of knowledge by way of a unique experience that consists, quite simply, in being psychoanalyzed. After that, you can talk. Being able to talk does not mean that you do talk. You could. You could if you wanted to, and you would want to if you were talking to people like us, people who are in the know, but what's the point? And so, we remain silent with those who do know and those who don't know, because those who don't know cannot know.

Then came things that were more complex, but they were always introduced with the greatest simplicity.

This volume brings together three lectures, which I have edited and which have not previously been published in book form. They are the following:

2 [André Isaac, 'Pierre Dac' (1893–1975), Raymond Devos (1922–2006) and Guy Bedos (1934–) are three well-known French comics.]

- 'The Place, Origin and End of My Teaching' (Vinatier, Lyon, an asylum founded under the July Monarchy). The lecture is followed by a dialogue with the philosopher Henri Maldiney.
- 'My Teaching, Its Nature and Its Ends' (Bordeaux). A lecture to psychiatric interns.
- 'So, You Will Have Heard Lacan' (Faculty of Medicine, Strasbourg). The title is borrowed from the beginning of the lecture.

Jacques-Alain Miller

THE PLACE, ORIGIN
AND END OF MY TEACHING

I do not think I will give you my teaching in the form of a pill; I think that would be difficult.

Perhaps that will come later. That is always how it ends. When you have been dead long enough, you find yourself being summed up in three lines of a textbook – though where I am concerned, I'm not too sure which textbook it will be. I cannot foresee which textbooks I will figure in because I cannot foresee anything to do with the future of my teaching, or in other words psycho-analysis. We don't know what will become of this psychoanalysis. For my part, I do hope it becomes something, but it is not certain that that's the way it is heading.

You see from that that my title, 'The Place, Origin and End of My Teaching', can begin to take on a meaning that is more than just summative. What I am trying to do

3

is to let you in on something that is under way, that is in train, something that is unfinished and that will probably be finished only when I am finished, if I don't have one of those annoying accidents that make you outlive yourself. There again, I'm telling you I'm not heading in that direction.

It's like a well-constructed dissertation, with a start, a beginning and an end. 'Place', because we really do have to begin at the beginning.

1

In the beginning, there was not the origin. There was the place.

There are perhaps two or three people here who have some idea about this same old story of mine. Place is a term I often use, because there are often references to place in the field that my discourses – or my discourse, if you prefer – deal with. If you want to know where you are in that field, it is advisable to have what other and more self-assured domains call a topology, and to have some idea of how the support on which what is at stake is inscribed was constructed.

I certainly will not get that far this evening because I absolutely refuse to give you my teaching in the form of a little pill. 'Place' means something very different here from what it means in topology, in the sense of structure, where it is just a question of knowing whether a surface is a sphere or a ring, because what can be done with it is not at all the same. But that is not what this is about. 'Place' can have a very different meaning. It simply means the place I have come to, and which puts me in a position to teach, given that there is such a thing as teaching.

Well, that place has to be inscribed in the register of what is our common fate. You occupy the place where an act pushes you, just like that, from the right or the left, any old way. It so happens that circumstances were such that, truth to tell, I really did not think it was my destiny, and . . . well . . . I just had to grab hold of the thread.

It all revolves around the fact that the function of the psychoanalyst is not self-evident, that, when it comes to giving him his status, his habits, his reference, and even his place in the world, nothing is obvious, nothing is self-evident at all.

There are the places I talked about first: topological places, places that have to do with essence, and then there is your place in the world. You usually get to that place by pushing and shoving. In short, it leaves you some hope. No matter how many of you there are, you will always end up in a certain place, with a bit of luck. It goes no further than that.

So far as my place is concerned, things go back to the year 1953. At that time, in psychoanalysis in France, we were in what might be called a moment of crisis. There was talk of setting up an institutional mechanism to settle the future status of psychoanalysts.

All accompanied by big election promises. If you go along with Mr So-and-so, we were told, the status of psychoanalysts will quickly be granted all sorts of official sanctions and blessings – especially medical sanctions and blessings.

As is the rule with promises of this kind, nothing came of them. And yet something was set up as a result.

It so happened that this change did not suit everyone, for extremely contingent reasons. So long as things had not been settled, there could be – were – frictions, what we call conflicts.

In the midst of this commotion, I found myself, along with a number of others, on a raft. For ten years, we lived on, well, on whatever came to hand. We weren't completely without resources, weren't completely down and out. And in the midst of all that, it so happened that what I had to say about psychoanalysis began to have a certain import.

These are not things that happen all by themselves. You can talk about psychoanalysis just like that, bah!, and it is very easy to verify that people do talk about it like that. It is not quite so easy to talk about it every week, making it a rule never to say the same thing twice, and not to say what is already familiar, even though you know that what is already familiar is not exactly unessential. But when what is already familiar seems to you to leave a lot to be desired, seems to you to be based on a false premise, then it has very different repercussions.

Everyone thinks they have an adequate idea of what psychoanalysis is. 'The unconscious . . . well . . . it's the unconscious.' Nowadays, everyone knows there is such a thing as an unconscious. There are no more problems, no more objections, no more obstacles. But what is this unconscious?

We've always known about the unconscious. Of course there are lots of things that are unconscious, and of course everyone has been talking about them for a long time in philosophy. But in psychoanalysis, the unconscious is an unconscious that thinks hard. It's crazy, what can be dreamed up in that unconscious. Thoughts, they say.

Just a minute, just a minute. 'If they are thoughts, it can't be unconscious. The moment the unconscious begins to think, it thinks that it's thinking. Thought is transparent to itself; you can't think without knowing you are thinking.'

Of course, that objection no longer carries any weight at all. Not that anyone has any real idea of what is refutable about it. It seems refutable, but it is irrefutable. And that is precisely what the unconscious is. It's a fact, a new fact. We have to begin to think up something that can explain it, can explain why there are such things as unconscious thoughts. It's not self-evident.

No one has in fact got down to doing that, and yet it is an eminently philosophical question.

I will tell you from the outset that that is not how I set about it. It so happens that the way I did set about it easily refutes that objection, but it is no longer really an objection because everyone now is absolutely convinced on that point.

Well then, the unconscious has been accepted, but there again we think that a lot of other things have been accepted – pre-packaged and just as they come – and the outcome is that everyone thinks they know what psychoanalysis is, apart from psychoanalysts, and that really is worrying. They are the only ones not to know.

It's not only that they do not know; up to a point, that is quite reassuring. If they thought they knew straight-away, just like that, matters would be serious and there would be no more psychoanalysis at all. Ultimately, everyone is in agreement. Psychoanalysis? The matter is closed. But it can't be for psychoanalysts.

And this is where things begin to get interesting. There are two ways of proceeding in such cases.

The first is to try to be as *with it* as possible, and to call it into question. An operation, an experience, a technique about which the technicians are forced to admit that they have nothing to say when it comes to what is most central, most essential – now, that would be something to see, wouldn't it! That might stir up a lot of sympathy because there are, after all, a lot of things to do with our common fate that are like that, and they are precisely the things psychoanalysis is interested in.

The only problem is that, well, psychoanalysts have, as fate would have it, always adopted the opposite attitude. They do not say that they know in so many words, but they imply that they do. 'We know a bit about it, but let's keep quiet about that. Let's keep it between ourselves.' We enter this field of knowledge by way of a unique experience that consists, quite simply, in being psychoanalysed. After that, you can talk. Being able to talk does not mean that you do talk. You could. You could if you wanted to, and you would want to if you were talking to people like us, people who are in the know, but what's the point?

And so we remain silent with those who do know and with those who don't know, because those who don't know can't know.

After all, it is a tenable position. They adopt it, so that proves it's tenable. Even so, it's not to everyone's liking.

And that means that, somewhere, the psychoanalyst has a weak spot, you know. A very big weak spot.

What I have said so far may seem comical to you, but these are not weaknesses. It is coherent. Only, there is something that makes the analyst change his attitude, and that is where it begins to become incoherent.

The psychoanalyst knows perfectly well that he has to be careful not to surrender to his temptation, to his penchant, and in his day-to-day practice he does watch his step. Psychoanalysis in the collective sense, on the other hand, or psychoanalysts, when there's a crowd of them, a host of them, want it to be known that they are there *for the good of all*.

They are very careful, however, not to move straight from this 'good of all' to the good [*bien*] of the individual, of a particular patient, because experience has taught them that wishing people well [*bien*] all too often brings about the opposite effect. It is rather in their dealings with the outside world that psychoanalysts become close to being real propagandists.

No, insofar as they are represented as a profession, psychoanalysts absolutely want to be on the right side, on the winning side. And so, in order to prove that they are, they have to demonstrate that what they do, what they say, has already been found somewhere, that it has already been said, that it is something you come across.

When you come to the same crossroads in other sciences, you say something similar: namely, that it's not all that new, that you'd already thought of it.

And so we relate this unconscious to old rumours, and erase the line that would allow us to see that the Freudian unconscious has absolutely nothing to do with what was called the 'unconscious' before Freud.

The word had been used, but it is not the fact that the unconscious is unconscious that is characteristic of it. The unconscious is not a negative characteristic. There are lots of thing in my body of which I am not conscious, and that are absolutely not part of the Freudian unconscious. That the body takes an interest in it from time to time is not why the unconscious workings of the body are at stake in the Freudian unconscious.

I give you this example because I do not want to go too far. Let me simply add that they even go so far as to say that the sexuality they talk about is the same thing that biologists talk about. Absolutely not. That's sales patter [*boniment*].

Ever since Freud, the psychoanalytic crew have been propagandizing in a style that the word *boniment* captures very well. You have the good [*le bon*] and then you have the wishing them well [*le bien*] that I was telling you about just now. This really has become second nature for psychoanalysts. When they are amongst themselves, the issues

11

that are really at stake, that really bother them and that can even lead to serious conflicts between them, are issues for those who know. But when they are talking to people who do not know, they tell them things that are intended to be a way in, an easy way in. It's standard practice, part of the psychoanalytic style.

It's a tenable position. It is not at all within the field of what we can call the coherent, but, after all, we know a lot of things in the world that survive on that basis. It is part of what has always been done in a certain register, and it is not for nothing that I have described it as 'propaganda'. This term has very specific origins in history and in the sociological structure. It is *Propaganda fidei*. It's the name of a building somewhere in Rome where anyone can come and go. So, that's what they do, and that's what they have always done. The question is whether or not it is tenable where psychoanalysis is concerned.

Is psychoanalysis purely and simply a therapy, a drug, a plaster, a magical cure or indeed something that can ever be described as a cure? At first sight, why not? The only problem is that is certainly not what psychoanalysis is.

We first have to admit that, if that is what it was, we would really have to ask why we force ourselves to put it on, because, of all plasters, this is one of the most fastidious to have to put up with. Despite that, if people do commit themselves to this hellish business of coming to see a guy three times a week for years, it must be because it is of some interest in itself. Using words you do not understand, such as 'transference', does not explain why it lasts.

We are just outside the door. So I really do have to begin at the beginning if I'm not to talk more sales patter or pretend I thought you knew something about psychoanalysis. Nothing I am saying here is new. Not only is it not new, it's staring you in the face. Everyone quickly notices that everything that is said about psychoanalysis by way of explanation *ad usum publicum* is sales patter. No one can be in any doubt about that because, after a while, you can recognize sales patter when you hear it.

Well, you know the funny thing is that this is 1967, and the thing that began, roughly speaking, at the beginning of the century, or let's say four or five years earlier if we want to go a little further back, if we really want to call what Freud was doing when he was on his own 'psychoanalysis' – well, it's still here.

Despite all the patter, psychoanalysis is alive and well, and even enjoys a kind of respect, of prestige, a sort of presence-effect that is quite unusual, if we think of the demands made by the scientific mind. From time to time, those who are scientists get annoyed, protest and shrug their shoulders. But something still remains, so much so that people who are capable of making the most disparaging comments about psychoanalysis will at other times invoke some fact or other, some psychoanalytic principle or precept, cite a psychoanalyst, or invoke what is known about a certain experience, as though that were the psychoanalytic experience. It makes you think all the same.

There has been a lot of sales patter in history but, if we look very closely, none of it has gone for this long. There really must be something to it, something, something that psychoanalysis keeps to itself, something that gives it this dignity, gives it some weight. This is something that it keeps very much to itself, and in a position that I have sometimes called by the name it deserves: 'extraterritorial'.

It is worth thinking about. It is in any case the main entrance to the question I am trying to introduce here.

There are in fact still people who have no idea at all what psychoanalysis is, who are not part of it, but who have heard of it and who have heard such bad things about it that they use the term when they want to find a name for a certain way of operating. They'll turn out books for you called *The Psychoanalysis of Alsace-Lorraine* or *of the Common Market*.

That is a really introductory step, but it does have the virtue of stating very clearly, and with no more reference than is required, the mystery surrounding some of the words we use, words that have their own shock-effect, that make sense. The word 'truth', for example. What is 'the truth'?

Well, 'psychoanalysis' is one of those words. At first, everyone feels that it means something very special, and above all that truth is, in this case, articulated with a mode of representation that gives the word 'psychoanalysis' its style, and gives it its second job, if I can put it that way.

The truth in question is exactly the same as in the mythical image that represents it. It is something hidden in nature, and then it comes out quite naturally, emerges from the well. *It comes out*, but that isn't enough. *It speaks*. It says things, usually things we were not expecting. That's what we hear when we say: 'At last we know the truth about this business. Someone is beginning to come clean.' When we talk about 'psychoanalysis', I mean when we refer to this thing that lends it some weight, that is what we are talking about, including the appropriate correlative effect, which is what we call the surprise-effect.

One of my students said to me one day when he was drunk – he's been perpetually drunk for some time now because, from time to time in his life, there are things that get nailed to the cross – that I was like Jesus Christ. He was obviously taking the piss, wasn't he? Goes without saying. I have nothing at all in common with that incarnation. I'm more the Pontius Pilate type.

Pontius Pilate had no luck, and nor do I. He said a thing that is really commonplace and easy to say: 'What is truth?' He had no luck, he asked the question of Truth itself. That got him into all kinds of bother, and he does not have a good reputation.

I really like Claudel.[3] It's one of my weaknesses, because I'm no Catholic [*thala*].[4] Claudel, with the incredible divinatory genius he always had, gave Pontius Pilate a few more years of life.[5]

When Pilate went for a walk, he says, whenever Pilate walked in front of what we call, in Claudelian language of course, an idol – as though an idol were something repugnant, ugh! – well, because, I suppose, he had raised the question of the truth precisely where he shouldn't have done, in truth, every time he walked in front of an idol – pouf! – the idol's belly opened, and you could see that it was just a piggy bank.

Well, much the same thing happened to me. You have no idea what effect I have on psychoanalytic idols.

---

3   [Paul Claudel (1868–1955) was a famous French poet, playwright, essayist, diplomat and member of the Académie française.]

4   [Slang term for 'Catholic' derived from *ceux qui vonT A LA messe* ('those who go to mass').]

5   [The allusion is to Paul Claudel's play *La Mort de Judas; Le Point de vue de Ponce Pilate* (1934).]

Let's start again.

We obviously have to take things one step at a time. The first step is that of the truth. After what psychoanalysis has said about truth, or what they think it has said, since it began to talk, it no longer impresses anyone. Naturally.

When something has been said and said again enough times, it becomes part of a general awareness. As Max Jacob used to say, and I tried to reproduce it at the end of one of my *écrits*, 'the truth is always new', and if it is to be true, it has to be new. So you have to believe that what truth says is not said in quite the same way when everyday discourse repeats it.

And then there are some things that have changed.

The psychoanalytic truth was that there was something terribly important at the bottom of it, in everything that gets hatched up when it comes to the interpretation of the truth, namely sexual life.

Is that true or not true?

If it is true, we need to know if that was only because this was at the height of the Victorian age, when sexuality was as important a part of the life of each and every one as it now is of everyone's life.

But, all the same, something has changed. Sexuality is something much more public. In truth, I do not think that psychoanalysis had much to do with that. Well, let's argue that if psychoanalysis did have something to do with it, and that is precisely what I am saying, then this is not really psychoanalysis.

For the moment, the reference to sexuality is not at all in itself something that can constitute the revelation of the hidden I was talking about. Sexuality means all sorts of things, the papers, clothes, the way we behave, the way boys and girls do it one fine day, in the open air, in the marketplace.

Sa vie sexuelle should be written using a special orthography. I strongly recommend the exercise that consists in trying to transform the way we write things. *Ça vice exuelle*. It's come to that.

It's quite a revealing exercise, and it's also very topical. Monsieur Derrida has invented grammatology to entice people who are partial to such things, the ones who at the moment think that, just because linguistics has flung everything out, it's been a failure. We have to find applications for it. Try playing around with spelling; it's one way of dealing with ambiguities, and it's not entirely pointless. If you write the formula *ça visse exuelle*, you can get a long way, you'll see. That will shed some light on certain things, and it might spark something in people's minds.

The fact that *ça visse sexuelle* means that there is a lot of confusion about the subject of psychoanalytic truth.

Psychoanalysts are well aware of that, I must say, and that is why they concern themselves with other things. You never hear talk of sexuality in psychoanalytic circles any more. If you open them, psychoanalytic journals are the chastest things in the world. They no longer tell stories about fucking. They leave that to the dailies. They deal with things that have far-reaching implications for the domain of ethics, like the life instinct. Ah, let's take a very life-instinctual view of things, and don't trust the death instinct. You see, we are entering the great performance, a higher mythology.

There are people who really believe they're in control of all that, and they talk about it as though these were objects we handle every day, in which case the point is to strike a good balance between them, between tangency and the right intersection, and with the greatest possible economy of effort.

And do you know what the ultimate goal is? Gaining what they pompously call a strong ego, ego strength in the midst of all that and all the scientific instances that go with it.

And they succeed. They make good employees. That's what the strong ego is. You obviously have to have a resistant ego to be a good employee. They do it at every level, at the level of patients, and then at the level of psychoanalysts.

Even so, you have to ask yourself if the ideal end of the psychoanalytic cure really is to get some gentleman to earn a bit more money than before and, when it comes to his sex life, to supplement the moderate help he asks from his conjugal partner with the help he gets from his secretary. When a guy had had a few problems in that domain, or was just leading a hellish life, or had some of those little inhibitions you can have at various levels, in the office, at work and even – why not? – in bed, that was usually considered to be a good outcome.

When all that has been removed, when the ego is strong and at peace, when the obsession with tits and bums has signed its little peace treaty with the superego, as they say, and when the itch isn't too bad, well, everything is fine. Sexuality is very much a secondary issue in all that.

My dear friend Alexander[6] – and he was a friend, and he wasn't stupid, but given that he was living in the Americas, he answered the call – even said, basically, that sexuality should be regarded as a surplus activity. You understand: when you've done everything properly and when you pay your taxes regularly, then what's left is sexuality's share.

6   [Franz Alexander (1891–1964), Hungarian-born analyst and founder, in 1932, of the Chicago Psychoanalytic Institute.]

There must have been a mistake somewhere for things to have reached that point. Otherwise, there is no real explanation as to why it took such a huge theoretical facilitation before psychoanalysis could settle in, even set up its world headquarters there, and then inaugurate this extravagant therapeutic fashion. Why all the discourses, if that's what it was all about? Something really must be wrong. Perhaps we should be looking for something else.

We might begin by saying to ourselves that there really must be a reason why sexuality once took on the function of truth – if it was just once, the whole point being that it was not just once. After all, sexuality is not all that unacceptable. And once it took on that function, it kept it.

What it's all about really is within reach, or at least within the psychoanalyst's reach, and he bears witness to that fact when he talks about something serious and not about his therapeutic results. What is within reach is the fact that sexuality makes a hole in truth.

Sexuality is precisely the domain, if I can put it that way, where no one knows what to do about what is true. And when it comes to sexual relations, the question of what we are really doing always comes up – I won't say when we say to someone 'I love you', because everyone knows that only idiots say that, but when we have a sexual relationship with someone, when that leads to something, when it takes the form of what we call an act.

An act is not just something that happens to you just like that, a motor discharge, as analytic theory says all too quickly and all too often – even if, with the help of a certain number of artifices, various facilitations, or even thanks to the establishment of a certain promiscuity, we succeed in turning the sexual act into something that has, they say, no more importance than drinking a nice glass of water.

That is not true, as you quickly realize. Because the whole point is that sometimes you drink a glass of water and then get diarrhoea. It's not straightforward, for reasons that have to do with the essence of the thing. In this relationship, we ask ourselves, in other words, if you are really a man, if you are a man, or if you really are a woman, if you are a woman. It is not only your partner who asks him- or herself that question; you ask it too, everyone asks it, and it matters, it matters right away.

So when I talk about a hole in truth, it is not, naturally, a crude metaphor. It is not a hole in a jacket, it is the negative aspect that appears in anything to do with the sexual, namely its inability to aver. That is what a psychoanalysis is all about.

When things get off to that kind of start, we obviously can't leave it at that. If we start with a question like that, a question that is really topical and pressing for everyone, we can feel that what Freud called 'sexuality' takes on a new meaning from the very beginning.

Freud's terms come back to life, take on a different import. We even notice that they have a literary import, which is one way of saying how well they lend themselves, as letters, to manipulating what is at stake. The ideal is, of course, to take thing as far as I have begun to push them, by God. I've pushed the literary specialists to the point where they finally admit that you can succeed in creating language when you want to avoid ambiguity, or, in other words, when you reduce it to the literal, to algebra's little letters.

This brings us straight to my second chapter: the origin of my teaching.

2

So you see, it's the opposite of what I was just saying.

I told you that its place was an accident. At the end of the day, I was pushed into the hole we are talking about, and no one wants to stumble into that. The reason why I fight so seriously is that, once it has started, you can't stop just like that.

Now, on the subject of the origin, well it certainly does not mean what it might suggest to you on first hearing, namely when and why it began.

I am not talking to you about what they nobly call the origins of my thought or even my practice in theses from the Sorbonne and other Faculties of Arts. One well-intentioned individual wanted me to talk to you about Monsieur de Clérambault, but I won't talk to you about him, because that really would not do.[7]

Clérambault taught me things. He simply taught me to see what I had in front of me: a madman. As befits a psychiatrist, he taught me that by interposing a very pretty little theory between me and him, the madman: mechanicism, and that is the most worrying thing in the world when you think about it. When you are a psychiatrist, you always interpose something.

So, what we have in front of us is a guy who has what Clérambault called 'mental automatism', or in other words a guy who cannot make a gesture without being ordered to, without being told: 'Look, he's doing that, the little rascal.' If you are not a psychiatrist, if you simply have, let's say, a human, intersubjective, sympathetic attitude, it really must give you a hell of a shock when a guy comes along and tells you something like that.

A guy who lives that way, who cannot make a gesture without someone saying: 'Look, he's stretching his arm out, silly bugger', well that really is something fabulous,

7 [Gaëtan Gatian de Clérambault (1872–1934), French psychiatrist. Lacan worked under him in the later 1920s, and his studies of erotomania and mental automatism were a significant influence on his early work.]

24

but if you decree that it's the effect of a mechanism somewhere, of something that tickles your convolutions and, besides, something that no one has ever seen, you just see how you calm down. Clérambault taught me a lot about the status of psychiatrists.

I've naturally retained what he taught me about what he called mental automatism. A lot of people have noticed the phenomenon since, and have described it in much the same terms, but that does not mean that it's not priceless when you hear it from the horse's mouth. Having said that, Clérambault was very clear-sighted because the fact remains that no one before him had noticed the nature of this mental automatism. Why? Because psychiatrists veiled it even more heavily then. They sometimes even put so many 'faculties of arts' between themselves and their madmen that they could not even see the phenomenon.

Even today, we might see more, might describe hallucination in very different terms. Not really being a psychoanalyst is all it takes, and they are not psychoanalysts. And they are not exactly psychoanalysts to the extent that, even though they are psychoanalysts, they keep that noble distance between themselves and what even psychoanalysts still call mental patients. Oh, let's drop it.

As for the origin of my teaching, well, we can no more talk about that than we can about any other question of origins.

The origin of my teaching is very simple. It has always been there because time was born at the same time as what we are talking about. My teaching is in fact quite simply language, and absolutely nothing else.

For most of you, this is probably the first time you've heard anything to do with this, because I think, really, that a lot of people here have yet to enter the Age of Enlightenment. A lot of people here probably believe that language is a superstructure. Even Mr Stalin did not believe that.[8] He explained very clearly that, if they started out that way, things could get nasty, and that in a country I would not dare to describe as advanced – I probably will not have time to tell you why – that could have certain repercussions. It is very unusual for anything that happens in the university to have repercussions, because the university is designed to ensure that thought never has any repercussions. But when you've got the bit between you teeth, as happened somewhere in 1917, and when Marr stated that language was a superstructure,[9] that could have had certain repercussions and could, for example, have begun to change Russian. Just a minute,

8 [See J.V. Stalin, *Marxism and the Problems of Linguistics* (1950).]
9 [Nikolay Yakovlevich Marr (1865–1934), Russian linguist.]

Father Stalin sensed that all hell would break loose if they did that. You can see what kind of confusion they might get into. 'Not another word about it. Language is not a superstructure,' said Stalin – and on that point he was in agreement with Heidegger: 'In language man dwells.'

What Heidegger meant by saying that is not what I am going to talk to you about this evening but, as you can see, I have to sweep up in front of the monument. 'In language man dwells' . . . even when it's extracted from Heidegger's text, it speaks for itself. It means that language was there before man, and that is obvious. Not only is man born into language in precisely the way he is born into the world; he is born through language.

That has to designate the origin of what we are talking about. No one before me seems to have attached the least importance to the fact that, in Freud's first books, the essential books on dreams, on what they call the psychopathology of everyday life, on jokes, we find one common factor, and it derives from stumbling over words, holes in discourses, wordplay, puns, ambiguities. That is what backs up the first interpretations and the inaugural discoveries of what is involved in the psychoanalytic experience, in the field that it determines.

Open the book on dreams, which came first, at any page and you will see that it talks about nothing but things to do with words. You will see that Freud talks about them in such a way that the structural laws Mr de Saussure disseminated all over the world are written out there in full. He wasn't the first to discover them, but he was eager to transmit them, to provide a basis for the most solid work that is now being done under the rubric of linguistics.

In Freud, a dream is not a nature that dreams, an archetype that stirs, a matrix for the world, a divine dream, or the heart of the world. Freud describes a dream as a certain knot, an associative network of analysed verbal forms that intersect as such, not because of what they signify, but thanks to a sort of homonymy. It is when you come across a single word at the intersection of three of the ideas that come to the subject that you notice that the important thing is that word and not something else. It is when you have found the word that concentrates around it the greatest number of threads in the mycellum that you know it is the hidden centre of gravity of the desire in question. That, in a word, is the point I was talking about just now, the nodal point where discourse forms a hole.

I allow myself this prosopopoeia simply to make what I am saying comprehensible to those of you who have not heard it before.

When I express myself by saying that the unconscious is structured like a language, I am trying to restore the true function of everything that structures under the aegis of Freud, and that in itself allows us to see our first step.

It is because language exists that truth exists, as everyone can come to see.

Why should something that manifests itself as a living pulsation and that can happen at as vegetative a level as you like be more true than everything else? The dimension of truth is nowhere, for the very good reason that we are not just talking about a biological scuffle. Even if we introduce the dimension that is intended to deceive an adversary, what does an animal's display add to it? It is as true as anything else, precisely because the point is to get a real result, namely to catch out the other. Truth begins to be established only once language exists. If the unconscious were not language, what might be called the unconscious in the Freudian sense would have no privilege, would be of no interest.

Firstly, because, if the unconscious were not language, there would be no unconscious in the Freudian sense. Would there be something unconscious? Well, yes, the unconscious is all very well. So let's talk about it. This table is something unconscious too.

These are things that have been quite forgotten by the so-called evolutionist perspective. In that perspective, they find it quite normal to say that the mineral scale leads naturally to a sort of higher point where we really see consciousness coming into play, rather as though consciousness stood out against what I have just evoked. If all we have to do is think consciousness only in the form of the cognitive function that makes it possible for very highly evolved beings to reflect something of the world, why should it, of all the other functions attendant upon the biological species as such, have the least privilege? The idealists, who are people who have been called various pejorative names, have made the point very clearly.

It is not as though we didn't have serious terms to make the comparison. We have a science organized on a basis that is not at all what you think it is. Nothing to do with a genesis. We did not create our science by entering into the pulsation of nature. No. We played around with little letters and little figures, and they are what we use to build machines that work, that fly, that move around the world, that travel long distances. That has absolutely nothing to do with anything that has been dreamed up on the register of knowledge. This is a thing that has its own organization. Which finally emerges as its very essence, namely our famous little computers of all kinds, electronic or not. That's what the organization of science is.

It doesn't work all by itself, of course, but I can point out to you that for the moment, and until further notice, there is no way we can build a bridge between the most highly evolved forms of a living organism's organs, and this organization of science.

And yet, it's not entirely unrelated. There are lines, tubes and connections there too. But a human brain is so much richer than any of the machines we have managed to build so far. Why shouldn't we raise the question of why it does not function in the same manner?

Why can't we perform three billion operations, additions and multiplications, and other standard operations in twenty seconds the way a machine does, when so many more things are being moved around in our brains? Curiously enough, our brains sometimes do work like that for a brief moment. On the basis of everything we know, the brains of the retarded do work like that. The phenomenon of *idiots savants* who can calculate like machines is well known.

This suggests that everything to do with the way we think is, perhaps, the result of a certain number of language-effects, and that they are such that we can operate on them. I mean that we can build machines that are in some way an equivalent, but on a much shorter register then we might expect from a comparable productivity if we really were talking about a brain that functioned in the same way.

I am not saying all this in order to base anything firm on it, but just to suggest to you the need for a little caution, particularly where the function might seem to operate thanks to what they call 'parallelism'. Not so as to refute the famous psycho-physical parallelism which was, as we all know, shown to be bullshit a long time ago, but to suggest that the break should not be between the physical and the psychical, but between the psychical and the logical.

Now that we've reached this point, we begin to get at least some idea of what I mean when I say that it is imperative to call into question how things stand with language if we wish to begin to shed some light on what is going on with respect to the function of the unconscious.

Indeed, it may very well be true that the unconscious does not function in accordance with the same logic as conscious thought. In which case, the question is: which logic?

It still functions logically, and this is not a pre-logic. No, but it's a logic that is more supple, weaker, as the logicians say. 'Weaker' indicates the presence or absence of certain basic correlations on which the tolerance of that logic is based. A weaker logic is not less interesting than a stronger logic, in fact it is much more interesting because it is much more difficult to make it stick, but it holds up all the same. That logic may be of interest, and taking an interest in it may even be our express object as psychoanalysts, always assuming that there are a few psychoanalysts here.

Think about it in very crude terms for a bit. The language apparatus is there somewhere in the brain, like a spider. It has a hold.

That might shock you, and you might ask 'Oh come on, really, what are you talking about, where does this language come from?' I have no idea. I'm under no obligation to know everything. And besides, you don't know anything about it either.

Do not imagine that man invented language. You're not sure about that, you have no proof, and you've seen no human animal become *Homo sapiens* just like that, in front of your very eyes. When he is *Homo sapiens*, he already has that language. When they, and especially a certain Helmholtz, were good enough to take an interest in how things stood with linguistics, they refused to raise the question of origins. That was a wise decision. It does not mean that this is a prohibition we have to maintain for ever, but it is wise not to talk too much rubbish, and one always talks rubbish when it comes to origins.

That does not mean that there are not whole piles of praiseworthy books from which we can gain some highly amusing insights. Rousseau wrote about this, and some of my dear new friends of the École Normale generation, who are kind enough to lend me an ear from time to time, have published a certain *Essay on the Origins of Languages* by him. Great fun, I recommend it to you.

But you have to be careful about anything to do with psychoanalysis. Once you have an idea of the sort of dissociation I've tried to make you feel this evening, perhaps you will see the futility of Piaget's child psychology.

If you ask a child questions based on a logical apparatus, especially if you yourself are a logician – and Piaget was a good one – then it is scarcely surprising that you find this logical apparatus in the child you are questioning. You observe it there the moment it begins to bite, rises to the bait in the child, but to deduce from this that it is the child's development that constructs the logical categories is a *petitio principii,* pure and simple. You ask the child questions in the register of logic, and the child answers you in the register of logic. But don't imagine children enter the field of language that way at every level. They need time, that's for sure.

There is a gentleman, not a psychoanalyst at all, who has quite rightly pulled Monsieur Piaget up over this point. He was called Vygotsky, and he operated somewhere around St Petersburg.[10] He even survived the revolutionary ordeals for a few years but, given that he was a bit tubercular, he left us before he finished all he had to do. He noticed that, curiously enough, the child's

10   [Lev S. Vygotsky (1896–1934), Russian psychologist.]

entry into the apparatus of logic should not be seen as the result of some inner psychical development, but that, on the contrary, it should be seen as something similar to the way children learn to play, if we can put it that way.

He noted, for example, that children have no access to the notion of a concept, to what corresponds to a concept, before they reach puberty. Now, why should that be the case? Puberty does indeed seem to designate a category of a different kind to some harebrained idea of how cerebral circumvolutions begin to function. Vygotsky saw that very clearly in his experiment.

I cannot advance the function of the subject here, despite what they told in advance. They are exaggerating. Personally, I think you're listening to me very well. You're kind, more than kind, because kindness alone would not be enough to get you to listen properly.

So I don't see why I shouldn't tell you a few things that are a little more difficult.

3

Why have I introduced the function of the subject as something distinct from anything to do with the psyche?

I cannot really give you a theoretical explanation, but I can show you how this has to do with the subject's function in language, and that is a double function.

There is the subject of the utterance [*énoncé*]. That subject is quite easy to identify. *I* means the person who is actually speaking at the moment I say *I*. But the subject is not always the subject of the utterance, because not all utterances contain *I*. Even when there is no *I* – even when you say, 'It's raining' – there is a subject of the enunciation [*énunciation*], and there is a subject even when it can no longer be grasped in the sentence.

All this allow us to represent a lot of things. The subject that concerns us here, the subject not insofar as it produces discourse but insofar as it is produced [*fait*], cornered even [*fait comme un rat*], by discourse, is the subject of the enunciation.

This allows me to put forward a formula that I present to you as one of the most primordial. It is a definition of what we call the 'element' in language. It has always been called the 'element', even in Greek. The Stoics called it 'the signifier'. I state that what distinguishes it from the sign is that 'the signifier is that which represents the subject for another signifier', not for another subject.

All I am thinking of doing this evening is to try to get you a bit interested. I don't think I can do anything more than plonk it in your hand and say to you: 'You try to make it function.' Besides, you have been given a few clues here and there, because I have pupils who, from time to time, show how it functions.

The important point is that it requires the formal, topological admission, not that it matters much where it hangs out, of a certain table, if you like, that we will call 'Table O'. They sometimes also call it 'the Other' around here, when they know what I'm talking about: the Other, which takes a capital 'O' too. To the extent that we can identify it in terms of the workings of the subject, this Other is to be defined as the site of speech. This is not where speech is uttered, but where it takes on the value of speech, or in other words where it inaugurates the dimension of truth. It is absolutely indispensable to the workings of what we are talking about.

So we quickly notice that none of this can happen all by itself, for all sorts of reasons. The main one being that it so happens that the Other I am telling you about is represented by a living being of whom you may have things to ask, but there's no obligation. It suffices that the Other is the one to whom you say 'Please God that . . .', or whatever it may be, and that you use the optative or even the subjunctive. Well, this site of truth takes on a very different meaning. Just the utterance I have just spoken to you is enough to make you feel that.

This introduces us to the reference to a very special truth, namely that of desire. The logic of desire, a logic that is not in the indicative, has never been taken so far.

They've begun things they call 'modal logics', but they've never got very far with them, probably because they did not notice that the register of desire must of necessity be constituted at the level of Table O, or in other words that desire is always what is inscribed as a repercussion of the articulation of language at the level of the Other.

Man's desire, I said one day when I had to make myself understood – why shouldn't I say 'man', though it's not really the right word? – desire full stop is always the desire of the Other. Which basically means that we are always asking the Other what he desires.

What I am telling you is quite easy to handle and is not incomprehensible. When you leave here, you will notice that this is true. You simply have to think about it and formulate it as such. And besides, such formulae are always very practical, you know, because you can invert them.

A certain subject whose desire is for the Other to ask him – it's simple, we invert it, turn it upside down – well, there you have the definition of the neurotic. See how handy that can be when it comes to finding your direction. The only problem is that you have to look at it very, very closely. And that takes time.

You can go further, and you will immediately see why the religious [*le religieux*] has been compared to the neurotic.

The religious is not neurotic at all. He is religious. But he looks like a neurotic, because he too combines things around what really is the desire of the Other. The only difference is that, because this is an Other that does not exist, because it is God, we need proof. So we pretend the Other is asking for something. Victims, for example. That is why this gradually becomes confused with the attitude of the neurotic, and especially the obsessional neurotic. It looks terribly like all the techniques used in victimary ceremonies.

This is my way of telling you that these things are quite easy to handle, and that not only do they not go against what Freud said, they even make him quite readable.

That emerges from just a simple reading of Freud, so long as we are prepared not to read him through the perfectly opaque glasses psychoanalysts normally wear to set their own minds at rest. You just have to take things just a little bit further to see that we are getting on to very scabrous ground, and that sheds some new light.

The fact that we can see a link between the neurotic and the religious is no reason to jump to what might be a rather hasty conclusion by bracketing them together. You have to see that there is after all a nuance, know why it's true, how far it is true, why it isn't quite true. Poor Freud, there he was, he said, digging holes and trenches

39

and collecting objects like an archaeologist. Perhaps he was not very sure about what he was meant to be doing: should he leave things *in situ* or carry everything off right away for his shelf? This shows that there really is something veracious about the question for a new-style truth that began with Freud.

Let us go back to the desire of the Other.

If you have taken the time to construct desire properly, that is, on a language basis, relating it to what is its fundamental linguistic basis, which is what we call metonymy, you'll progress much more rigorously into the field to be explored: namely, the field of psychoanalysis. You may well even notice the true sinew of something in psychoanalytic theory that is still so opaque, so obtuse and so obstructed.

Whilst it is in the field of the Other that desire is constituted, and whilst 'man's desire is the desire of the Other', man sometimes fails to live up to his desire, meaning his own desire. Well, now that you have had some practice, you are in a position to see things less precipitously than at first, in ways that are less intent upon immediately finding anecdotal explanations. When man's desire has to be extracted from the field of the Other and has to be my desire, well, something very funny happens. Now that it is his turn to desire, he notices, well, that he is castrated.

That is what the castration complex is. It means that something necessarily happens in significance, and it is that sort of loss which means that, when man enters the field of his own desire insofar as it is sexual desire, he can do so only through the medium of a symbol that represents the loss of an organ insofar as it takes on, in the circumstances, a signifying function, the function of the lost object.

You will say that I am now advancing something that is no more transparent for that. But I'm not looking for transparency, I am trying, first of all, to stick to what we find in our experience, and if it is not transparent, well that's too bad.

First, we have to accept castration. We're obviously not used to doing so. It makes it difficult to recover that transparency, to get it back. And so we make up all sorts of cock and bull stories, including stories about the threats made by our parents, who are supposedly to blame. As though the fact that our parents said something of the kind were all it took to give rise to a structure as fundamental and as universal as the castration complex.

It's reached such a point that women are inventing one for themselves, inventing a phallus they can demand, just so as to be able to consider themselves castrated, which is precisely what they are not, poor little things, at least where the organ – the penis – is concerned, because they do not have one at all.

Even so, I'm going to say something that will calm you down, make it a little more comprehensible for you.

The reason why castration exists is, perhaps, quite simply that desire – when it really is a question of our desire – cannot have been, cannot be, something we have, cannot be an organ we can handle. It cannot be both being and having. So, the organ serves, perhaps, a purpose that functions at the level of desire. It is the lost object because it stands in for the subject *qua* desire. Well, it's a suggestion.

On this point, you can set your minds at rest. Above all, don't imagine that there is something daring about this. The point is to try to formalize correctly what is no more than the experience we have to verify day by day.

We have students who come to tell us stories about their parents, and who finally notice not only that we can understand patients with this language of Lacan's as easily as we can with the language that is spread and diffused by institutions established on a different basis; we actually understand them better.

Patients sometimes say some very clever things, and it is Lacan's own discourse that they are speaking. Only, if psychoanalystis hadn't heard Lacan first, they wouldn't even have listened to the patient, and would have said: 'Just another mental patient talking more nonsense'.

Right. Let's turn to the end.

4

The end of my teaching. When I use the word 'end', I do not mean the end of the world. I am not talking about the day it snuffs it; no, the end is the *telos*, why I do it.

The end of my teaching is, well, to train psycho-analysts who are capable of fulfilling the function known as the subject, because it so happens that it is only from this point of view that we can really see what is at stake in psychoanalysis.

'Psychoanalysts who are capable of fulfilling the func-tion of the subject' may not seem all that clear to you, but it's true. I will try to outline to you what we can deduce about it from the theory of the training analysis.

Doing a bit of mathematics would not be bad training for psychoanalysts. In mathematics, the subject is fluid and pure, and it isn't stuck or trapped anywhere. It would help them, and they would see that there are cases in which it no longer circulates, precisely because, as you saw just a moment ago, the Other seems to be split between the site of truth and the site of the desire of the Other. It's the same with the subject.

A post-language subject; that is the subject we can purify so elegantly in mathematical logic. Only, there is still always something to be cited, something that was already there. The subject is manufactured by a certain number of articulations that have taken place, and falls from the signifying chain in the way that ripe fruit falls. As soon as he comes into the world he falls from a signifying chain, which may well be complicated or at least elaborate, and what we call the desire of his parents is subjacent to that very chain. It would be difficult not to take that into account in the fact of his birth, even, and especially, when it was, precisely, a desire for him not to be born.

The least we can ask might be for psychoanalysts to notice that they are poets. That's what's funny, very funny, about it. I will take the first example that comes to mind.

I'm making some use of the notes I made on the train for your benefit. My paper wasn't the only one on the train. There was a copy of *France-Soir* lying around, so I glanced at it.

Claudine, you know, that pretty French girl, I don't know if she was strangled or stabbed, but in any case there was an American who quickly disappeared, and now he's in a mental home, much good that will do him.

Let's think about it. He's in a mental home, and a psychoanalyst goes to see him. It does happen, because he is a member of a very good society. So what do we find? We find LSD. Seems he was as high as a kite when it happened.

LSD, but even so, even so, LSD can't completely mess up the signifying chains. Or at least let's hope we find something acceptable. We find what they call a murderous impulse, and we find that it is perfectly articulated with a certain number of signifying chains that were quite decisive at one moment or other in his past.

Oh come on, it's the psychoanalyst who is saying that. Why not just say he bumped the girl off, and be done with it? It is true we notice that there were causes somewhere at the level of the signifying chain. The psychoanalyst says so, and the really funny thing is that we believe him.

I beg your pardon, they believe him. If we don't believe him, we're poorly thought of, we're out of touch. We just have to understand what believing him means. I am not of course counting on the kindness of English judges. That should at least encourage the psychoanalysts to be somewhat critical of something quite analogous when it comes to, for instance, the transference. The psychoanalyst says that the transference reflects something that happened in the past. That's what he says. The rules of the game say that we have to believe him. But why should we, when all's said and done? Why shouldn't what is now happening in the transference have its own value? Perhaps we should find another mode of reference to justify the preference that is given to the psychoanalyst's point of view when it comes to what actually happened.

I'm not the one who came up with that idea. An American psychoanalyst – they are not all stupid – has just made exactly these comments in a relatively recent issue of the *Psychoanalytic Gazette* [*Journal officiel de la psychanalyse*].

I want to end with living things, as they say. So here is a little example. 'If I'd known', said one of my patients, 'I'd have wet the bed more than twice a week.'

I'll spare you what led up to him coming out with that. It came after a whole series of considerations about various privations, and after he had cleared some of the debts he felt he was burdened with. He felt quite at ease, and rather oddly regretted the fact that he had not done so earlier.

So, you see, one thing in particular strikes me: the psychoanalyst does not realize the decisive position he holds by articulating, *nachträglich*, as Freud puts it, a deferred action that establishes the truth of what came earlier. He does not really know what he is doing in doing that.

'Retroactively' [*après-coup*] . . . you can find it in the first pages of a certain vocabulary that came out not so long ago. I needn't tell you that no one would ever have included this 'deferred action' in a Freudian vocabulary if I hadn't brought it out in my teaching.[11] No one before me had ever noticed the importance of this *nachträglich*, even though it is there on every page of Freud. And yet it is very important to detach the 'retroactively' in this case.

No psychoanalyst had thought of this, I mean ever written this, even though it is directly in line with what he does as a psychoanalyst. When someone tells us 'God in heaven, why didn't I wet the bed more than twice a week?', if you know how to listen, it means that the fact of only wetting the bed twice a week has to be taken into consideration, and that we have to take into account that the figure 2 is introduced in correlation with the neurotic symptom.

Perhaps knowing how to use what is nothing more than an effect of thought's internal coherence is enough. When thought is not too empirical, it does not consist in standing and gaping, and waiting for inspiration to come from the facts.

And besides, how can we even say that we are dealing with facts, with facts pure and simple, in a situation as articulated, as interventionist, and as artificial as

11   [See the entry on 'Deferred action; Deferred' in J. Laplanche and J.-B. Pontalis, *The Language of Psychoanalysis*, trans. Donald Nicholson-Smith (London, 1973). The French original was published in 1967.]

psychoanalysis? The fact that the psychoanalyst never moves and keeps quiet three-quarters of the time, or ninety-nine point nine per cent of the time, does not mean we have to see it as an exercise in observation. It is an experiment in which the psychoanalyst is involved, and no psychoanalysts would ever dare to try to deny it. Only, you have to know what is going on. Less so here than anywhere else, we cannot fail to recognize that the real mechanism behind a scientific structure is its logic, and not its empirical side.

Once we realize that, we might perhaps begin to see something. And perhaps the psychoanalyst would be all the more keen on feeling good about himself if he could be more than just a psychiatrist.

It so happens that there is no reason why we should restrict O's famous little *d* – that desire of the Other – to the field of analytic practice alone. Whilst there is no such thing as a collective consciousness, we might perhaps note that the function of the desire of the Other really does have to be taken into consideration when it comes to the organization of societies, especially these days.

This outcome results from the institution of what is usually called communism, namely a desire of/for [*de*] the Other based upon justice in the redistributive sense of the word. We might note more than one correlation, with the subject of science on the one hand, and, on the other, with what happens at the level of the relationship with truth. Wouldn't it be interesting to try to see the correlation between putting the desire of the Other in charge of a regime, and the fact that the done thing is to obstinately defend an ever-growing number of outright lies?

Don't get the idea that my remarks are directed against the commies. That's not what I mean at all. And I am going to give you another riddle. Do you think that things are any better on the other side, where the desire of the Other is based upon what they call freedom, or in other words injustice? In a country where you can say anything, even the truth, the outcome is that, no matter what they say, it has no kind of effect whatsoever.

I would like to end there, in order to tell you that there may come a time when we find that being a psychoanalyst means having a place in society.

That place will, I hope, I am sure, be taken, even if it is for the moment occupied only by psychoanalysts who have lurched into their little joke shop.

Psychoanalysis obviously might be a mode, a scientific mode of approach concerning things to do with the subject. It will, however, become more and more useful to preserve it in the midst of the ever-accelerating movement in which our world is entering.

DISCUSSION

Henri Maldiney: How can we discuss your discourse? We would have to do so via a plurality of points and slip into its articulations, and we cannot do that for everything. I will ask you a simple question about the distinction between your two subjects.

It seems to me that you over-simplify the first, the one that, precisely, has no lexical meaning, the one that is determined solely by the act of speaking, the one that is not simply determined by all the word's possible semantemes, which are never pure, as it happens, nor by the set of morphemes, but by the possibilities inherent in a situation.

It seems to me that, because you overlook that, you find yourself in disagreement with Heidegger, whom you just cited, because Heidegger's *archè* is basically a presence or articulation that exists prior to any morphological structure, before it becomes a meaning. It is primarily sovereign in the concrete and outside the understanding, in the situation itself. So long as the *I* that speaks and the *you*, the alterity it needs, requires . . . because if everything is clear, there is nothing left. What I mean is that, if the other does not resist, the *I* cannot locate itself.

Now, the *I* that is so instituted escapes the legislation

of language, except in the logic of preaching, and it appears to me that, because of the logic of your exposé, and by defining the subject of the enunciation, you do enter into a logic of preaching. Now, the logic of preaching is after all no more than one form of logic, and it is surely a logic of the object rather than of the subject/object relationship.

More specifically, the objectivation present in that logic seems to me to be quite the opposite of any notion of *insight* because it is no more than the second stage in the singularization of a much more fundamental function, namely that of being-in-the-world. Now, being at the very heart of this logic and being-in-the-world are not the same thing at all. You are in danger of remaining within the field of the taken-for-granted, to talk like Husserl.

And in relation to the thing, the very articulation of things, which is always present in Heidegger, I don't really see what presence it can have, if language really does become the sign, or what I would call the very form of the absolute, beyond the reality principle, which is the opposite of Freud's *Verneinung*, which you make . . .

J.L.: I've not said a single word about *Verneinung* today.

Henri Maldiney: No, and yes, given that the repression is not removed by the intellectual meaning of the representation, and that it is meaning we obtain through language. It seems to me that language itself is not contemporary, and is not just born of time. In general, language does without time, and meaning is basically reversible. And it is only in the present that you can recuperate that something that is not simply in meaning . . .

J.L.: Say no more, please. I claim to follow Heidegger only to the extent that I allow myself to cite him in order to find a striking formula. Even assuming that some people in my audience even thought of that connection, I immediately said that I was borrowing that formula, and that's what I did here. What Heidegger does with it is a different matter.

On the other hand, and to respond to what appears to me to be the real point you are making, I don't really see why you say that I sacrifice the subject of the articulation, of the *archè*, of the situation of the subject insofar as it speaks and hears to the extent that it enters into the present situation *qua* being-in-the-world, as you say, because that is precisely why I speak of the 'division of the subject'.

I am saying that the subject, whilst it remains the subject, functions only when divided. Indeed, that is the whole import of what I establish. I have to tell you that I consecrate this division of the subject, denounce it and demonstrate it in very different ways than reductive way I have used here and which, as it happens, certainly does not correspond to the division itself. I would have to have done something I absolutely refuse to supply the reference this evening, because you must not think that I have been talking about what, with your permission, I will call, to save time, not just my teaching but my doctrine, and everything that follows from it. I have not been able to do that.

There is a causal element in this division, and it is what I call *objet petit a*. There are those who have already heard about this, and there are those who have not. It may look like a strange thing to those who have not heard about it, especially as I have not really had time to evoke the order it might belong to, and because it is closely related to the structure of desire. At all events, this *objet petit a* is in the very place where that singular phallic absence is revealed, at the root of what I have tried here to put in the centre because it is the centre of the analytic experience, namely what I, like everyone else, call castration.

So in order to say that the subject was divided, I simply indicated its two positions in relation to the subject of language. Our subject as such, the subject that speaks, if you like, may well claim primacy, but it will never be possible to regard it purely and simply as the free initiator of its discourse, simply because, being divided, it is bound up with that other subject – the subject of the unconscious, which happens to exist independently of any linguistic structure. That is what the discovery of the unconscious is.

Either this is true, or it is not true. If it is true, that should stop even M. Heidegger from always talking about how matters stand with the subject in the same way. And besides, if we get involved in the Heideggerean controversy, I would be so bold as to suggest that Heidegger's use of the term 'subject' is far from being homogeneous.

Henri Maldiney: He hardly ever uses it.

J.L.: Precisely. I do.

Henri Maldiney: You have your reasons.

J.L.: I have my reasons, and I am trying to articulate them for you now. Along the same lines, you raised a certain number of objections by introducing a few registers of Freudian doctrine, repression, *Verneinung*, and a lot of other things. It is quite obvious that all that has played its role, and has been sifted through my thinking for the last seventeen years, I'm sorry, ever since it's been going on . . . what I came here to introduce, or rather evoke by way of the three references I call, successively, the 'place, origin and end of my teaching'. The objections that you might raise, and which are naturally still very present, arise from a certain perspective. I am well aware of what you intend to preserve by raising them, if only because demonstrating that to you would surely require a much longer dialogue than the one we can have here.

Henri Maldiney: I am not denying what you say about the unconscious. In the same way that you turn it into a language, Husserl turns it into 'inactualities'. We therefore cannot have a dialogue, but, let's call it just a double monologue.

J.L.: That's not specific to what goes on between philosophers. It's the same between husband and wife.

*MY TEACHING,
ITS NATURE AND ITS ENDS*

I agreed to visit a psychiatric clinic because I had good cause to presume that it was not without reason that I had been asked to take part in what we call in modern jargon a *colloquium*.

Not bad, that term. I quite like it. We talk together, in the same place, I mean. That does not necessarily mean that we think. Each of us talks because we are in the same place: we co-loquate. 'Colloquium' is an unpretentious term, unlike the term 'dialogue'. Being in dialogue is one of the most enormous pretensions of our times. Have you ever seen people in dialogue? Occasions when we speak of dialogue are always a little bit like domestic quarrels.

So I was hoping to co-loquate. But given that there are so many of you, that will be much more difficult than I thought.

The fact is that I have prepared nothing that is especially intended for you. If I had come here to say something in front of you and found only silence in your presence, I would feel that I was imitating the woman sowing seeds [*la semeuse*].[12] But just because you are sitting in rows does not mean that they are furrows, and nor does it mean that the seeds are sure to find soil where they can grow. That is why I would like some of the people who are sitting on the tiers in this room to be good enough to ask me a question.

It's highly unlikely, of course, but that is the request I am making, as I do whenever, and it is not that often, I happen to speak in a context that is, it has to be said, unfamiliar to me, because I do not think many of you have been following what I teach.

1

What I teach has caused something of a stir.

That dates from the day – and thank God I put it off for as long as I could – I collected together something I had to call *Écrits*, in the plural, because it seemed to me that that was the simplest term to designate what I was going to do.

12 [*La semeuse*: the female figure of the sower that appeared on some (pre-Éuro) French banknotes.]

I brought together under that title the things I had written just to put down a few markers, a few milestones, like the posts they drive into the water to moor boats to, in what I had been teaching on a weekly basis for twenty years or so. I don't think I repeated myself much. I'm quite sure I didn't, because I made it a rule, a sort of imperative, never to say the same things more than once. That, I think you will agree, is quite a feat.

In the course of those long years of teaching, from time to time I composed an *écrit* and it seemed to me important to put it there like a pylon to mark a stage, the point we had reached in some year, some period in some year. Then I put it all together. It happened in a context in which things had gained ground since the time when I started out in teaching.

I was speaking for the benefit of people it concerned directly, for the specific people who call themselves psychoanalysts. It had to do with their most direct, most day-to-day, and most urgent experience. It was done expressly for them, and it's never been done for anyone else. But it is true that it had occurred to me that it might be of interest to people to whom it was not addressed and whom it did not concern at all. Any production of this nature always has an exemplary character to the extent that it faces up to a difficulty you can sense, a real thing, a concrete thing, to use another fashionable word. Even if

61

you do not understand it very well, reading what I have written has an effect, holds your interest, is of interest. It is not that often that you read an *écrit* that is necessarily something urgent, and which is addressed to people who really have something to do, something it is not easy to do.

It is primarily for that reason, I suppose, that, if we approach them from a different angle, we can agree to consider these *Écrits* unreadable; people at least pretend to read them, or to have read them. Not, naturally, the people who supposedly do that for a living, or in other words the critics. Reading them would force them to prove their worth by writing something that might at least have something to do with what I am advancing, but at that point they become suspicious. As you may have noticed, this book has not had many reviews. Probably because it is very thick, difficult to read, obscure. It is not designed for everyday consumption at all. You might say to me that that remark might suggest I'm making excuses. It might mean that I'm saying I should have produced a book for everyday consumption, or even that I'm going to. Yes, it is possible. I might try to. But I am not used to that. And it is by no means certain that it would be a success. Perhaps it would be better if I did not try to force my talent. And I do not find it particularly desirable in itself, because what I teach will indeed eventually become common currency. There will be people who will get down to it, who will put it about. That is obviously not quite the same thing, and it will be a bit distorted. They'll try to introduce it into the hubbub. They will do all they can to reposition it in relation to a certain number of those very solid convictions that suit everyone in this society, as in any society.

I have no intention of making criticisms of the society in which we live here. It is no better and no worse than any other. Human society has always been a folly. It's none the worse for that. It has always been like that, will always be like that. After all, it has to be admitted that a fair number of ideas are increasingly spineless. Everything is a continuation of everything else. It even ends up making each and every one of us feel a bit sick. At lunch just now, in the little circle of people who have given me such a kind welcome, we were talking about what they call TV, the thing that allows you to catch up with the world scene at any moment, to keep up with everything cultural. Nothing cultural will escape you any more.

While we're on the subject, I would like to draw your attention to a major difference, which has perhaps not been emphasized enough, between man and the animals. It is worth mentioning precisely because we forget about it. I am talking about a difference in the context of nature because I really do not want to dabble in cultural anthropology.

Unlike what happens at every level of the animal kingdom – which starts with elephants and hippos and ends with jellyfish – man is naturally characterized by the extraordinary embarrassment he feels about – what should we call it? By the simplest name we can find, by God – the evacuation of shit.

Man is the only animal for whom this is a problem, and it's a prodigious one. You don't realize, because you have little devices that evacuate it. You have no idea where it goes afterwards. It all goes through pipes and is collected in fantastic places you have no idea of, and then there are factories that take it in, transform it and make all sorts of things that go back into circulation through the intermediary of human industry, and human industry is a completely circular industry. It is striking that there is not, to my knowledge, any course on political economy that devotes a lesson or two to it. This is a phenomenon of repression which, like all phenomena of repression, is bound up with the need for decorum. Trouble is, we don't really know which decorum.

There is a man of wit I met a very long time ago, and I'm sorry I didn't know him better. He's quite well known. Aldous Huxley. He was a charming man, of good family, and he wasn't entirely stupid, not at all stupid in fact. I don't know if he is still alive. Get hold of his *Adonis and the Alphabet*. There's a French translation, published by Stock, if memory serves. The title obviously does not announce the chapter it contains on what I've just been talking about: waste disposal.

Talking about this is always shocking, even though it has always been part of what we call civilization. A great civilization is first and foremost a civilization that has a waste-disposal system. So long as we do not take that as our starting point, we will not be able to say anything serious.

Amongst those people we have for some time called primitive, though I have no idea why we call them that because they have none of the characteristics of primitiveness at all, or let's say the societies that social anthropologists study – even though, now that the theoreticians have put their oar in and go on about the primitive, the archaic, the pre-logical and all that bullshit, no one understands them any more – well, there are few problems with waste disposal. I am not saying there aren't any. And perhaps it is because they have fewer of these problems that we call them savages, or even noble savages, and we regard them as people who are closer to nature.

But when it comes to the equation *great civilization = pipes and sewers*, there are no exceptions. There were sewers in Babylon, and Rome was all sewers. That's how the City began, with the *Cloaca maxima*. It was destined to rule the world. So we should be proud of it. The reason why we are not is that, if we gave this phenomenon what we might call its fundamental import, we would find the prodigious analogy that exists between sewage and culture.

Culture is no longer a privilege. The whole world is more than covered in it. Culture clots on you. Because we are cooped up in the great shell of waste that comes from the same place, we make vague efforts to give it a form. What does that come down to? To great ideas, as they say. History, for example.

It comes in handy, does history. It doesn't have just one meaning; it has a thousand and one meanings. There are people who look to it as a support. Not that they would bother to see what Hegel has to say on the subject, of course. There were others before him, Bossuet, for example. He put everything in the hands of Providence. That at least was clear. I have to say that I have a high opinion of the *Discourse on Universal History*. First, because it was that that inaugurated the genre, and it did so on the basis of clear principles. It is God who pushes the pawns across the board. That really does deserve to be called 'history' [*histoire*]. Everything revolves around the story [*histoire*] of what happened to a certain gentleman. Not bad, it gave other people an appetite for it and made history much more profound. I'm not saying that all these ideas are unacceptable, but some funny use has been made of them.

Don't let that make you believe that culture is a goal of which I disapprove. Far from it. It discharges. It completely discharges us from the function of thinking. It discharges us from the only thing that is of any minor interest in that function, which is quite inferior. I fail to see why we should confer any kind of nobility upon the phenomenon of thinking. What do we think about? About things over which we have absolutely no control, things that we have to turn over, over and over again, turn over seventy times in the same direction before we manage to understand them. That's what we call thinking. As I cogitate, I agitate, rummage around. It only begins to get interesting when it takes responsibility, when, in other words, it comes up with a solution, as formalized a solution as possible. If it does not come up with a formula, a formalization, as mathematical a solution as possible, we cannot see the interest, or the nobility. We don't see why it's worth dwelling on.

The point of history is to write the history of thought, I mean, to get rid of the little efforts, timid efforts but, truth to tell, they're often scrupulous – that's what survives best – that this one or that one has made to solve certain problems. As a result, our professors would be very embarrassed about having to draw a line and say what they think of the logic of Descartes or a few of those strays, to say whether it holds up – more to the point than whether its bloody time is up – but it's much easier to do the history of thought, which comes down to looking for what they have passed on from one to another. It's fascinating, especially when it's bullshit, and when you see the sort of thing that has survived.

The mechanism I am pointing out to you works in a very contemporary way. It is not theory, and I am not here to make a big thing of theory. You can see that with your own eyes, without going to university, where that is in fact what they teach when they say they're doing 'philosophy'.

You know the nonsense they've come up with now. There is structure, and there is history. The people they've put in the 'structure' category, which includes me – it wasn't me who put me there, they put me there, just like that – supposedly spit on history. That's absurd. There can obviously be no structure without reference to history. But first, you have to know what you are talking about when you talk about history. I will try to tell you something about it.

It is always difficult to pin down what is going on in the field of what we are really cogitating without any

misunderstandings. The words have often been sur-
rounded by all sorts of confusion for a little too long.
That is what now allows some people to use historical
reduction, which has nothing to do with historical rights,
so to speak, with the function of history. So they come
out with questions that have to do with, not structure,
but what they call structuralism.

For example, in the course of a conversation that
preceded my appearance before you, someone, someone
very respectable as it happens, said to me: 'Couldn't you
say how you, what you do, what you advance, relates to
structuralism?' I replied: 'Why not?' So let's set things
out properly and trace the process.

The function of what we call a cultural trend is to mix
and homogenize. Something emerges and has certain
qualities, a certain freshness, a certain tip. It's a bud.
The said cultural trend kneads it until it becomes completely reduced, despicable, and communicates with
everything.

It has to be said that this is not satisfactory, despite
everything. Not for reasons to do with any internal
necessity, but for commercial reasons. When it has
been uprooted, it becomes exhausted. Although I've
been using bad language I think I can take the liberty of
repeating the formula that occurred to me in this
connection. Eating shit is all very well, but you can't

always eat the same shit. So, I try to get hold of some new shit.

The origins of this new fashion, of what you call 'structuralism', lie in the attempts to lump together men who do not easily fit into their categories, who've stayed in the smallest room. You would have to study all the processes, all the resistance functions that left them isolated, and then associated, assimilated them, stuck them together. I've had the insane good luck to be one of them, and I feel fine about it. These are people who went about things a little more seriously. Well done, Lévi-Strauss. They won't be able to do as well as that in the future, that's for sure. It's overwhelming. And then there are others. They change them from time to time.

For the moment, they are making a serious effort to get all that into general circulation, really trying. Oh yes, it's not a bad solution. Until now I've held out against this operation, because they don't quite know what to make of what I'm saying. They don't know because, with good reason, they really have no idea of what it concerns, even though it seems to them that it's something like that. They have to struggle to resorb it like they do with everything else, but they don't know how to.

They'll find a way. Especially if I help them.

2

It is obvious that what I teach has to do with what we call the psychoanalytic experience.

They want to transport all that into, I don't know, something that doesn't put it in any position to know, what they call by a nice name that sounds like a sneeze, a *Weltanschauung*. Far be it from me to be so pretentious. That's what I hate most. I'll never indulge in that, thank God. No *Weltanschauung*. And all the rest of those *Weltanschauungen,* I loathe them.

What I teach has to do with something very different, with technical procedures and formal details concerning an experience that is either very serious, or an incredible errancy, something mad, demented. And that is what it looks like from the outside. The basic thing about analysis is that people finally realize that they've been talking nonsense at full volume for years.

For my part, I try to show, by starting out from what clarifies its *raison d'être*, why it lasts, why it goes on, why it ends up as something that is very often not at all what they think they have to announce to the outside world, what they claim to owe to the way it operates. It's obvious that this is a discursive operation, a discourse-operation. You'll say to me that some people go through their whole analysis without saying anything. If that's the case, it's an eloquent silence.

We did not have to wait for analysis to take an interest in discourse. Indeed, discourse is the starting point for anything scientific. It's not enough to imagine philosophy in the register I was just telling you about, namely how beautiful thoughts were passed on down the ages. That is not what this is about. The purpose of philosophy is to specify the extent we can extract things that are certain enough to be described as science from a discourse-operation.

It's taken time for a science to emerge: our science, which has certainly proved its worth – though what it proves remains to be seen, though it has proved effective. It's all about perfecting the correct use of discourse, and nothing more.

And what about experience, you say? The whole point is that experience is constituted as such only if we start out by asking the right question. We call that a hypothesis. Why a hypothesis? A hypothesis is simply a question that has been asked in the right way. Something, in other words, begins to take a de facto form, and a fact [*fait*] always made up of [*fait de*] discourse. No one has ever seen a received fact. That is not a fact. It's a lump, something you bump into, all the things that can be said about something that is not already discursively articulated.

Psychoanalysis, which is an absolutely new example of discourse, leads us to take another little look at how we pose the problem of, for example, roots. It encourages us, for example, to investigate the phenomenon constituted by the appearance of a logic, its adventures and the strange things it ends up showing us.

There was a certain Aristotle, and his position – what you believe after this declaration is of little importance – was not dissimilar to mine. We don't really have much idea of what, of whom he had to deal with. They were called, in a vague, confused way, sophists. We naturally have to be suspicious of these terms, and we have to be very careful. There is in fact a black-out on what people got from the sophists' oracle. Probably something effective, because we know that they paid them very well, in the same way they pay psychoanalysts. Aristotle certainly got something out of it, but it had absolutely no effect on the people he was talking to. That's how it was for him, and how it is for me. It's the same. What I say makes no difference to psychoanalysts who are already very settled in their ways. But we can continue, continue, and hope.

All the wonderful things we find in the *Prior Analytics*, the *Posterior Analytics* and the *Categories* are what we call logic. It's been devalued now because we are the ones who do real, serious logic, though we've not been doing it for long; since the mid-nineteenth century, about 150 years.

Correct, strict, true logic is the logic that began with a certain Boole. It gives us the opportunity to revise a few ideas. We always believed that, when we had established a few good principles from the outset, everything we could derive from them would run smoothly and that we would always fall on our feet. The important thing was that a system should not be contradictory. That was all there was to logic. And then we notice that it is not like that at all. We discover lots of things that escape us. If by some chance a few people here and there have heard of a certain Gödel, they may know that even arithmetic turns out to be a basket; I'm not saying it is double-bottomed, but there are lots and lots of holes in the bottom. Everything disappears through the hole in the bottom.

That is interesting, and it is not impossible that taking an interest in it might not be without a formative value for someone like a psychoanalyst. But for the moment it gets us nowhere, because we have here a very particular problem that I call the age question. If you want to do logic, or anything else to do with modern science, you have to start before you have been completely cretinized, by culture of course. Obviously, we are always a little cretinized because there is no escaping secondary school. Of course, secondary school may have its value too, because those who survive it and still have a real scientific vivacity are cases apart, as anyone will tell you. My good friend Leprince-Ringuet, [13] who was cretinized at the

13 [Louis Leprince-Ringuet, French physicist (1901–2000).]

same time as me at school, escaped immediately, brilliantly and in lively fashion. It took psychoanalysis to get me out. It has to be said that not many people have taken advantage of it the way I have.

Logic is a fairly precise thing and requires some mental resilience that has not been completely worn down by all the stupid things they force down your throat. So I must have had it at a very early age. The only problem is that being very young is not the best condition to make a good psychoanalyst either. And when someone with some experience does happen to enter the psychoanalyst's profession, it is too late to teach him the key things that would train him for its particular practice.

I mentioned logic to give you a target. There's more to it than that, but logic is exemplary if we take it at *Stotle*'s level, because he obviously did try to inaugurate something. Of course those people, the sophists, were already using logic, and in quite astonishing, very brilliant, very effective ways, at one level of rationality. That they themselves did not give it its name obviously does not mean that that isn't what it was, that's for certain. They would not have been so good at enticing citizens, and non-citizens, and at giving them tips on how to win debates or on how to debate the eternal questions of being and non-being, if it didn't have a formative effect. *Stotle* tried to perfect a technique, what they call the

Organon. He gave birth to a line, to a line of philosophers, and now you can see where that got him: his line has died out a little bit, now that philosophy has come down to meaning the history of thought. Which means we're having a bloody hard time of it. Fortunately there are still a few counterfeiters around to try to put you back on top of things. They're called phenomenologists.

Psychoanalysis gives us a chance, a chance to start again.

3

As I think I have got across to you, there is the closest relationship between the emergence of psychoanalysis and the truly regal extension of the functions of science. Although it may not be immediately apparent, there is a certain relationship of contemporaneity between the fact of what has been isolated and condensed within the analytic field, and the fact that, everywhere else, only science still has something to say.

That, you will tell me, is a scientistic declaration. Of course it is, and why shouldn't it be? And yet, that is not quite what it is, because I do not add what we always find on the fringes of what is conventionally called scientism, namely a certain number of articles of faith to which I by no means subscribe. There is, for example, the idea that all this represents progress. Progress in the name of what?

One objection was put forward to me just now, and it comes, it seems to me, from certain corners where they label themselves psychoanalysts. I have to say that it inspired me. It was passed on to me by a lady who had, I'm told, given a lecture on what Lacan is on about. Thanks, basically, to her, I can let myself go a little. If I understand rightly, the objection in question might be formulated thus: 'Why do you find it necessary to drag in the subject? Where is a trace of the subject in Freud?'

That was a terrible blow, I can tell you. The terrible thing is that after a time – time that I waste – there is a growing gulf between you and the effect of culture, of journalism. Now that I am in the public eye, I need an intermediary to tell me where some people might be at. So they think that dragging in the subject in connection with Freud is something new, an invention.

At this point, I am sincerely invoking anyone who is not a psychoanalyst, not that there can be many psychoanalysts here. Anybody who knows just a little about what we are talking about knows that Freud talks about three things.

The first is that it [*ça*] dreams.[14] So it's a subject, isn't it? What are we all doing here? I have no illusions about

14 [The play is on *le ça: das Es*, the id.]

this: an audience, even a qualified audience, is dreaming while I'm struggling away. Everyone is thinking about his own business, the girlfriend you're going to meet later, the piston rod that's just gone on your car, something that's gone wrong somewhere.

And there again, it gets things wrong. Think of the slips of the tongue, the bungled actions, the very text of your existence. They make a grotesque farce of what they've always trotted out to you about the ideal functions of consciousness and all that implies about the person who has to gain control. I don't know what it's about. You can see in my *Écrits* my stupor when I read the things that my dear friend Henri Ey, [15] and I love him, has dreamed up. He wanted to civilize psychiatrists, so he invented organo-dynamism, and it's a complete shambles that makes no sense at all. I defy anyone to see any connection between what we are dealing with, the text of the subject, and whatever it is that he has dreamed up about this so-called synthesis, the construction of the personality, and I don't know what else. Where are they, these constructed personalities? I don't know, I'm looking for them with a lighted lamp, like Diogenes. The beautiful thing about it is that, despite all the appeals that are made to these constructs, they actually fail. That

15   [Henri Ey (1900–1972), French psychiatrist.]

means something. It's always the others who succeed. There are even people in the room who have got to their feet. For my part, I've succeeded in going to bed.

Third, it [*ça*] dreams, it fails, and it laughs. And are those three things subjective, or are they not, I ask you? We have to know what we are talking about. People who wonder why I needed to drag in the subject when we are dealing with Freud have absolutely no idea what they are saying. I have to conclude that that's where they are at, though I thought the resistance was based on something more sophisticated.

The subject in question has nothing to do with what we call the subjective in the vague sense, in a sense that muddles everything up, and nor does it have anything to do with the individual. The subject is what I define in the strict sense as an effect of the signifier. That is what a subject is, before it can be situated in, for example, one or another of the people who are there in an individual state, even before they exist as living beings.

Of course we can say in conventional terms, 'It's a good or bad subject, it's a moral subject, it's the subject of consciousness', or whatever you like. This idea of a subject of knowledge really is a load of nonsense, and one wonders how they can go on talking about it in philosophy classes at school. It can mean only one thing: that anything that is alive knows enough, just enough to survive. But there's nothing more to be said about it. That can be extended to the animal kingdom or – and why not? – the vegetable kingdom.

As for the idea of relating what they call man to what they call the world, that would mean regarding that world as an object and turning the subject into a correlative function. If we think of the world as an *ob-ject*, we assume the existence of a *sub-ject*. That relationship can only become substance, essence, thanks to a great image of contemplation whose completely mythical character is obvious. We imagine that there were people who contemplated the world. There are obviously things like that in Aristotle, for instance when he is talking about the spheres, but this simply means that there is no theory of the celestial spheres that does not involve a contemplative movement.

We know what a science is. None of us can master the whole of science. It steams ahead at full speed under its own impetus, does science, so much so that there is nothing we can do about it. Those who are most in the know are also those who are the most embarrassed about it.

All possible enlightened experience indicates that the subject is dependent on the articulated chain represented by science's acquired knowledge. The subject has to take his place there, situate himself as best he can in the implications of that chain. He constantly has to revise all the little intuitive representations he has come up with, and which becomes part of the world, and even the so-called intuitive categories. He's always having to make some improvements to the apparatus, just to find somewhere to live. It's a wonder he hasn't been kicked out of the system by now.

And that is in fact the goal of the system. In other words, the system fails. That is why the subject lasts. If something gives us the feeling that there is a place where we can lay hands on it, where it's the subject we are dealing with, then it's at the level known as the unconscious. Because it all fails, laughs and dreams.

It only dreams, fails and laughs in a perfectly articulated way. What is Freud constantly doing in his approach, his discovery, his revelation of what the unconscious is all about? What does he spend his time on? What is he dealing with? No matter whether it is the text of the dream, the text of the joke or the form of the slip, he is manipulating articulations of language, of discourse.

In the margins of a small etching by Goya, we find written: 'The sleep of reason produces monsters.' It's beautiful and, as it's by Goya, it is even more beautiful – we can see the monsters.

You see, when you are talking, you always have to know when to stop. Adding 'produces monsters' sounds good, doesn't it? It's the beginning of a biological dream. It took biology a long time to give birth to science too. They spent a long time dwelling on the calf with six hooves. Oh! Monsters, all that, the imagination! We love it. Oh, it's so fine. You know, the psychiatrists tell us that it's teeming, swarming with psychopaths, that it invents and imagines things. It's fantastic. They are the only ones to imagine that. I cannot tell you how it is for the psychopath – I'm not enough of a psychopath – but it is certainly not the way the psychiatrists imagine it to be, especially when they talk about, I don't know, the physiology of sensation, or of perception, and then move on to constructs and then generalizations, all so they can think about what they will come up against, poor things. That has absolutely nothing to do with their constructs. That much should be obvious.

So you have to know when to stop. *The sleep of reason* – that's all. So what does that mean? It means that reason encourages us to go on sleeping. Once again, I don't know if there is any danger of you understanding a little declaration of irrationalism on my part. No, no, quite the opposite. What we would like to get rid of, to exclude, namely the reign of sleep, finds itself annexed by reason, its empire, its function, by the hold of discourse, by the fact that man dwells in language, as someone said. Is it irrationalism to notice that, or to follow reason's line of thought in the text of the dream itself? It's possible for a whole psychoanalysis to go by before what might well happen does happen: we've reached the point where we wake up.

Somewhere Freud writes *Wo Es war, soll Ich werden*. Even if we remain at the level of his second topography, what is this, if not a certain way of defining the subject? Where the reign of sleep was, I must come, become, with the special accent the verb *werden* takes in German, and we have to give it its import of becoming in the future. What does that mean? That the subject is already at home at the level of the *Es*.

There is no point in quibbling and saying that, in his second topography, Freud calls a certain system the perception-consciousness system, *das Ich*, with the article because there are no words in German that function the way *moi* and *je* function in French. *Das Ich* is something like the other two agencies, to use that vague term, he associates it with: the *Es* and the *Überich*. What is it, if not, strictly speaking, the core of the subject?

It might even have to do with that grotesque, ridiculous function all those who were for a while my fellow-travellers pounced upon, and they came from God knows where, and full of psychology, which is no preparation for psychoanalysis. I am talking about the function of inter-subjectivity. Ah! Lacan, the 'Rome Discourse', 'Function

and Field of Speech and Language', intersubjectivity!
There is you and there is me, and we say so to each
other, send each other things, and so we are intersubjective. All that is purely confusional.

I think you know my position on this point but, if you
don't, I am in a position to get it across to you better.
Confusing the subject with the message is one of the great
characteristics of all the stupid things that are said about
the so-called reduction of language to communication.
The communication function has never been the most
important aspect of language. That was my starting point.

Von Frisch thinks that bees have a language because
they communicate things to one another. That is just the
sort of thing that people say from time to time when the
fancy takes them: namely, that the fact that something
comes to us from them proves that we receive messages
from starry bodies. In what sense is that a 'message'? If
we give the word 'message' a meaning, there must be a
difference between that and the transmission of whatever
it might be. If there wasn't, everything in the world
would be a message. And besides, there's a sense in
which everything is a message, given what makes the
functions of the transmission and conveying of information fashionable, as they say. It is not difficult to see that
this information can be so formalized as to inscribe it as
the very opposite of signification. That in itself is enough

to show that information, understood in that sense, is not to be confused with the result of what is conveyed in the use of language.

The articulation of language calls into question, first of all, the issue of the subject of the enunciation. The subject of the enunciation is definitely not to be confused with the one who takes the opportunity to say of himself *I*, as subject of the utterance. When he has to talk about himself, he calls himself *I*. It simply means *I who am speaking*. The *I*, as it appears in any utterance, is nothing more than what we call a *shifter*. Linguists claim that it is also the subject of the enunciation. That is quite wrong, whatever they may say. It is so wrong that it has obviously been untrue ever since we have known it. You can always try to find the subject of some enunciations. It is not, in any case, there for anyone who can say *I*.

This means, all the same, that we have to reconstruct the so-called communications schema a little bit. If there is one thing that has to be called into question, it is the simple function of intersubjectivity, as though it were a simple dual relationship between a sender and a receiver that worked all by itself. It's not that at all.

The first thing involved in communication is knowing what it means. Everybody knows that. You don't need much experience to show that what the other is saying obviously never coincides with what he says.

That is also why you work yourself to death trying to construct a logic for the same. So that there will be no doubts surrounding the little signs you can put on the board. Precisely: you are trying to eliminate the subject. And once you have put down some little letters, the subject is indeed eliminated for a moment. You will naturally find the subject once more when you get to the end, in the shape of all sorts of paradoxes. That is the demonstrative and fascinating thing about logic's attempts to study things closely.

Someone will object that, if we want to speak of something that is absolutely not psychical, but that is a real metapsychology, or in other words something very different from a psychology, we have to talk about the id, the ego or the superego. We act as though all that were obvious, self-evident, quite natural, something we could see coming a mile off. Nothing of the kind. Not only is it different from all the old waffle; if there is something that we can legitimately call an intersubjectivity, an intersubjectivity that is not just dramatic but tragic, then it has nothing to do with the order of communication, with an intersubjectivity of people who push and shove, get jammed up against each other and suffocate each other – well, it takes the form of the id, the ego and the superego, and it can easily do without what you would call a subject.

They ask me why I talk about the subject, why I supposedly add that to Freud. That is all that gets talked about in Freud. But it gets talked about in a brutal, imperative way. It is a sort of bulldozer operation, and it brings back to life everything that they have been trying to cover up about the subject for thousands of years of the philosophical tradition.

As I was telling you just now, it is in just that order of things that they are now up to something. What I have stressed, and I cannot claim to be doing anything more than suggesting a dimension here, has indeed a counterpart, and it is supplied by philosophers. There is, for example, one to whom I make a brief allusion in the first issue of my journal *Scilicet*, a very talented boy who still has a few rehashes in store for us when it comes to great classical themes, and I knew of their existence long before I first met him at a congress. So, he said to me: 'All that's very well, I agree with what you say' – and indeed it was obvious that he did agree, since in his article on Freud he wrote nothing that I had not said already – but what I've said, 'But why, why, do you insist on calling it the subject?'

That's the way it is when you touch on certain topics, you find that someone has already laid claim to them. One of the people who is just learning that lesson dared to write a book on Racine one day. The trouble was, he wasn't the only one, because there was someone else who thought he was the expert on Racine. How dare he? And so on. In this case, the philosopher was quite prepared to say to me: 'Why do you keep calling the unconscious – an unconscious you say is structured like a language – the subject?'

When analysts ask me questions like that, I'm shocked but I can't say that I am surprised. But coming from philosophers, they are so disconcerting I can't find any answer, except to say: 'I keep the subject . . . to get you talking.'

And yet, it would be quite insane not to retain the term. Some happy accident in the philosophical tradition has perpetuated the line that began with Aristotle's *Organon*, which I was talking about just now. Read, or reread, the *Categories*, my little friends, or those of you who from time to time get it into your heads to read something other than textbooks, and you will see from the start the difference between the subject and sub-stance.

This is something that is so crucial that the two thousand years of philosophical tradition I was talking about have been trying to do just one thing, trying to resorb that. The man who is regarded as the pinnacle of the philosophical tradition – Hegel – suggests with, I have to say, dazzling brilliance, something that negates what we touch upon in dreams, namely that substance is already the subject, before it becomes the subject, as we saw just now with Freud's formula.

It all starts with the initial trauma of Aristotle's assertion, which introduced the most rigorous divorce between subject and substance. That has been completely forgotten.

That the subject has outlived the philosophical tradition demonstrates, if we can put it that way, that we really are behaving like intellectual failures.

Is that not a reason not to abandon the term 'subject', now that the time has finally come to invert its usage?

SO, YOU WILL HAVE HEARD LACAN

I cannot say that my situation is very difficult. On the contrary, it is extraordinarily easy. The very way I have been introduced indicates that I will, at any rate, have spoken in my capacity as Lacan.

So, you will have heard Lacan.

The 'lecture' is not my style. It is not my style because, every week for the last fifteen years, I have given something that is not a lecture, but what they used to call a seminar in the days when there was some enthusiasm, and it is a class, but it is still a seminar, still goes by that name.

It is not I who will testify to the fact, but the few who have been there from the start, with some replacing others: not one of those classes has ever been repeated.

There was a moment, in the course of circumstances when I thought I owed it to the few who were around me to explain something to them, something that we will be dealing with now. And, my God, that something must be sufficiently broad for me still not to have finished explaining it to them.

It's strange. Perhaps it is also that the very development of what I had to explain caused me problems and raised new questions. Perhaps. But it's not certain.

Be that as it may, I make absolutely no claim to be evoking even its main detours today, even by way of allusion for the benefit of those who know what I am talking about, and who even have some idea of what I have said about it.

As for the rest of you, and I suppose you make up part of this gathering, who know little or nothing about it, giving you even some idea of it is out of the question, assuming that what I have just said is true, namely that I have never repeated myself.

In truth, the 'lecture' genre presupposes a postulate that is essential to the very name 'university': there is such a thing as a universe, by which I mean a universe of discourse. Discourse, that is to say, has apparently succeeded for centuries in constituting an order that is sufficiently established for everything to be compartmentalized, divided into sectors that we have only to study carefully and separately, with everyone making his own little contribution to a mosaic whose frames are already adequately established because enough work has already been done on them.

It takes only a quick look at history to contradict the idea that the strata that have been laid down throughout history, and terraced over a period of centuries, constitute assets that add up and that can therefore come together to create that university – the University of Letters, the *Universitas Litterarum* that is basic to the teaching that bears the name.

Do not, I beg you, understand the word 'history' to mean what you are taught under the name of 'history of philosophy', or of whatever else it is, because that replastering job is designed to delude you into thinking that the various stages of thought engender one another. You have only to take a quick look at history to see that this is far from being the case and that everything originates, on the contrary, in breaks, in a succession of trials and openings that have at every stage deluded us into thinking that we could launch into a totality.

The outcome is that you only have to go into any bookseller's shop, any antiquarian bookshop, and pinch any book from the time of the Renaissance. Open it, read it properly, and you will see that you won't be able to follow the thread of three-quarters of the things that preoccupied them and seemed essential to them. On the other hand, what might seem obvious to you came into being during a certain epoch, and it was not twenty, thirty or fifty years ago, but dates to no further back than Descartes.

It was from Monsieur Descartes onwards that certain things happened, and they are certainly worthy of note, especially the inauguration of our modern science, a science whose distinguishing feature is the somewhat compelling efficacy that allows it to intervene in the most everyday details of everyone's life. But in truth, perhaps it is that that distinguishes it from earlier bodies of knowledge, which were always more esoteric practices, by which I mean that they were thought to be the privilege of a small number.

For our part, we are immersed in the findings of that science. Even the most banal things here, even the funny little chairs you are sitting on, are actually products of it. In the past, they used to make chairs with four feet, like sturdy animals; they had to look like animals. Nowadays they look just a little mechanical. And of course you still have not got used to them, and you miss the chairs of old.

So, what I teach concerns something that was born at a moment in history and in the centuries when we were already up to our necks in the context of science, even before we could say it in the way I have just said it. I refer to psychoanalysis.

I have been led to put myself in a very particular position as a teacher, as my position consists in starting again at a certain point, in a certain field, as though nothing had been done. That is what psychoanalysis means.

That is because nothing had been done within a certain classical field hitherto known as 'psychology', and because that can of course be explained by all the historical conditions that had gone before. What I mean is that, whilst a very elegant construct that served certain purposes, assuming a certain number of basic postulates, had been elaborated, it so happened that those postulates always had to be reconstructed retroactively. If, basically, we accept those postulates, everything is fine, but if something about them is radically called into question, nothing works any more.

My teaching does not serve that purpose, but that is what it is enslaved to. It serves, and serves to promote something that happened, and that something has a name: Freud.

It sometimes so happens that things that happen do have a name. That in itself is a problem, and it certainly cannot be solved with the help of notions such as those we call influences, borrowings, substance. In many cases, knowing what the sources are can be of some use. It actually is of some use at the literary level, at the level of and in the so-called *Universitas litterarum* perspective. But it resolves absolutely nothing when something that has some existence suddenly emerges – a great poet, for example. Trying to approach the problem in the name of sources is pure madness.

The 'sources' point of view can also be of use in day-to-day teaching, or in what I just called the 'lecture' genre. The only problem being that breaks do occur from time to time, that there are people who have indeed been able to borrow little bits from here and there to nurture their discourse, if only the essence of that discourse that starts out from a breaking point.

If my teaching serves to promote Freud and declares itself to be in his service, what, in that case, do sources mean? They mean, of course, that what interests me is not reducing Freud to his sources.

I will, on the contrary, demonstrate the function he served as a break. When, of course, it comes to bringing him back into line, putting him back in his place within general psychology, there are others who are trying to do that, as a result of which they overlook the only thing that is interesting, namely why Freud is a name to which there clings that very singular thing that gives that name its place in the consciousness of our era.

After all, why does the name Freud have a prestige similar to that of Marx without ever having had, to date, any of his cataclysmic repercussions? Why the devil not? Why is there a whole field where we can do nothing but evoke him, and where it even has the value of a nodal point – irrespective of whether or not we agree with what he said, and what his message appears to be, without being able to say strictly what it means, other than that it is a sort of mythology that is in circulation. How is it that this name is so present in our consciousness?

That I am trying in this way to promote Freud is a very different matter from what I will call the victories of thinkers. Of course it is not unrelated to thought, but it is something that enlightens us as to what may already be surprising about the incidence of the effects of thought on the history we share.

You might think that, given that it is doctors who bear the burden of Freud's message for the moment, it might be said that, after all, he is less important than the concrete things they are dealing with, and I mean concrete in the sense the word has as a resonance, things that are made that way, a bit, a block, something to do with – come on, we all know it – with their patients, who are said to be just things to be treated, something that resists.

Freud taught us that some of these patients [*malades*] are intellectually ill [*malades de la pensée*]. The only

99

problem is that we have to pay attention to the function that is so designated. Are they *malades* in the sense that we say that 'he's a bit wrong in the head', in the sense that it is all that takes place at the level of thought? Is that what it means?

That, basically, is what was said before Freud. Indeed, that is the whole problem. We speak of 'mental psychopathology'. There are several floors inside the organism, and there is an upper floor. Somewhere at the command level, there must be a guy in a little room from where he can switch off everything up there in the ceiling. That is what we imagine thought to be, from a certain summary viewpoint. Somewhere, there is something directive, and if things go wrong up there, we will have mental problems. If everything is turned off, there will obviously be some disruption, but we will still be alive and well, stumble blindly to a door and start all over again. That is the classic conception of intellectual illness.

The expression 'sick in the mind' can be understood on a different register. We can speak of 'animals that are sick in the mind' [*animaux malades de la pensée*] in the same way that we speak of 'animals that are sick with the plague'.[16] It's another acceptation. I am not going to go so far as to say that thought in itself is an illness. In itself,

16   [The allusion is to La Fontaine's seventeenth-century fable *Les Animaux malades de la peste*.]

the plague bacillus is not an illness either. It causes illness. It causes it in animals that are not designed to tolerate it, to tolerate the bacillus. Perhaps that is what it is all about. Thinking is not an illness in itself, but it can make some people ill.

Be that as it may, what Freud initially discovered is something like that. At the level of illness, there are thoughts that circulate, even ordinary thoughts, our bread and our wine, the thought that we share to some extent, and of which it might be said: 'Think one another.' That is the thought we are talking about. Certain phenomena that constitute a certain field of illnesses, the field of the neuroses, have a great deal to do with this 'Think one another'. And that is how Freud introduces himself.

A tradition that called itself — and why not? — philosophical has it that the process of thought is an autonomous function or, to be more accurate, that it is situated, constituted, only when it gains its autonomy from that ladder, from the human pyramid built by climbing on one another's shoulders that allowed, over a period of centuries, the emergence of the preconditions for the pure exercise of thought, and they have to be isolated if thought is to get a new and very different grip on everything it first had to preserve itself from in order to guarantee that it was being properly exercised.

This process is certainly not nothing because it seems that it eventually generated that which is our privilege: a proper physics. But in the way it is represented to us – the work of culture and isolation leading in the direction of a certain efficacy – completely ignores the question of the human animal's relationship with thought. Now, the human animal is involved with thought from the very beginning, and it seems certain that, even at the most elementary, physiological level, in the sense that the word designates the most familiar functions, those functions are already involved with thought functions in their maintenance capacity, in their capacity as something that is circulated, displaced.

In a word, the work of the philosophers gave us to suppose that thought is a self-transparent act, that a thought that knows it is thinking is the ultimate criterion, the essence of thought. Everything we thought we should purify ourselves of, rid ourselves of, in order to isolate the process of thought, namely our passions, our desires, our anxieties, and even our colics, our fears, our follies, all that seemed simply to bear witness to intrusion within us of what someone like Descartes calls the body because, at the cutting edge of this purification of thought, we find that there is no point at which we can grasp that thought is divisible. It all stems from the way the passions interfere with the workings of our organs. That is the point we reach at the end of one philosophical tradition.

Freud says quite the opposite. He makes us go back, he tells us that it is at the level of our relations with thought that we have to look for the mechanism behind a whole region – which, it seems, expands to an unusual extent, in the context of our civilization – of governance by the prevalence, the increase in thought that is in some way embodied in what they call *brains-trusts*. Thought has always been embodied, and we are still aware of that in what seems to be eminently redundant, scrappy and unassimilable, at the level of certain failings that, apparently, seem to owe nothing to anything but the deficit function. It thinks, in other words, at a level where it does not grasp itself as thought at all.

It goes further than that. The reason why it [*ça*] thinks at a level where it cannot grasp itself is that it does not want to grasp itself at any price. It would rather relinquish itself than be thought; there's no question about it. There is much more to it than that: it is not at all willing to accept observations that might come from outside to encourage that which thinks to grasp itself as thought. That is what the discovery of the unconscious is.

That discovery was made at a time when nothing was less open to challenge than the superiority of thought.

The people they called, in certain registers, the noble, civilized descendants of the Greeks and Romans, in particular, saw themselves as men who had finally reached the stage of positive thought, and placed what history has demonstrated to be an excessive trust in the progress of the human mind and in the fact that in certain zones, you could cross a frontier and enter the circle of those men in the world who could call themselves enlightened, with a little help, if you were given a helping hand.

To Freud's credit, he noticed that we had to take a different view long before history reminded us that we should be more modest. History showed us this, which we have been able to grasp fully every day since such and such a date, namely that there isn't some kind of privileged area within the human field, defined as the field of people who have the singular ability to handle language. Whether they are civilized or not, people are capable of the same collective enthusiasms, the same passions. They are always at a level that there is no reason to describe as higher or lower, as affective, passionate or supposedly intellectual, or developed, as they say. The same choices are available to all of them, and they can translate into the same successes or the same aberrations.

Although it has been greatly diminished by being passed on by the offices of the more or less disabled people who are his official representatives, the message Freud brings is definitely not discordant with what has happened to us since his day, and that should inspire us to take a much more modest view of the possibility of progress in thought.

Freud is not discordant at all; he is still there with his message, and its incidence is perhaps all the stronger in that it is still in the firmest, most enigmatic state, even though they have managed to give it a certain buoyancy thanks to a certain level of vulgarization. At the level where a human being is a thought that fortunately contains within it a secret warning of which it is unaware, people feel that there is in Freud's message, even in the form in which it circulates for the moment, now that it has been transformed into pills, something precious though no doubt alienated – but we know that we our bound up with that alienation; because it is our alienation.

Anyone who takes the trouble to try to get back to the level where this message has some effect is sure to be of interest – and the point has been made, if only by the collection of dross known as my *Écrits* – sure to be of singular interest to the widest variety of people, to the most widely scattered people, the most strangely situated people and, in a word, everyone.

This is to the astonishment of those who insist that literature should always respond to certain needs. They wonder why my *Écrits* are selling. I'm a nice guy, so when a journalist comes along and asks me that question, I put myself in his position and tell him: 'I'm just like you, I don't know.' And then I remind him that these *Écrits* are no more than a few threads, floats, islands or markers that I put down from time to time for the people I'm teaching. I've put the pill away somewhere safe, so that they remember that I'd already said that at such and such a time.

But the *Écrits* are of interest to the journalist after all, and he tells me that people are definitely reading them. Perhaps it is because of what I say in them that they are of interest to so many people. At the 'need' level, concrete need of course, which is the principle behind all advertising, one is surprised. Why should they need these *Écrits* which are, it seems, incomprehensible? Perhaps they need to have a place from which they can see that they're talking about something they do not understand. Why not?

Whilst the goal of my teaching is to promote Freud, it obviously does not do so at the 'general public' level. The general public does not need me to promote Freud. They get by perfectly well with what the others, my pals, are doing. As I have just explained to you, whatever we do and even if we hand responsibility over to the guild of psychoanalysts – and I am one of the jewels in its crown –

make what you like, or even what I like, of that, Freud is definitely there.

Until now, the effort of my teaching has therefore not consisted in promoting Freud at the level of the popular press. There would be no need for it, and in truth I don't see why I should have made it my concern or made the effort, if it were not addressed to psychoanalysts.

What I give you is this, in its broadest formula.

I really have to take the view that thought exists at the most radical level, and already conditions at least a vast part of what we know as the human animal.

What is thought? The answer does not lie at the level where they take the view that its essence is being self-transparent and knowing that it is thought. It is, rather, at the level of the fact that every human is born steeped in something we call thought, but further investigation obviously demonstrates, from Freud's earliest work onwards, that it is quite impossible to grasp what it is about unless we base ourselves on his material, as constituted by language in all its mystery.

I say 'mystery' in the sense that no light has been shed on its origins, but that something can, on the other hand, certainly be said about its conditions, its apparatus, and about how a language is made at the minimal level of what we call its structure.

To deny that Freud started out from that is to deny the obvious, to deny what becomes obvious to us from his first great works, especially the *Traumdeutung*, *The Psychopathology of Everyday Life* and the *Witz*, which we have translated as *Jokes*. Freud first designates the field of the unconscious in phenomena that look irrational and capricious, that bob up and down like floats: dreams are absurd, slips of the tongue are ridiculous and the *Witz* that make us laugh without knowing why are pathetic.

I have to be quick.

Whilst Freud directs us towards the field of sexuality as something that is especially implicated in all these phenomena, the fact remains that the structure and material in question designate the unconscious, because all this happens without any help at all from what we previously took for thought, or in other words something that was able to grasp itself as conscious. That is indeed Freud's starting point and the inversion he introduces.

This raises some completely new questions.

The first question is whether consciousness itself is that thing that claims to be perhaps the most imponderable, but certainly the most autonomous of things, and whether the unconscious might be just an inference, a detail – and a detail that acts like a mirage – compared with how matters stand with the effects of a certain radical articulation, the articulation we grasp in language, to the extent that it is perhaps what generates the something that is in question under the name of thought.

Thought, in other words, is not to be conceived as a kind of flower that peeps through at the top of some evolution or other, and it is difficult, after all, to see what the common factor might be that destines it to produce that flower. Our task is to take a serious look into what its origins might be.

Thought certainly does not, in any case or for the moment, appear to us in the form of a function that can in any sense be described as higher. On the contrary, it is a precondition into which we fit as best we can a whole series of animal functions, from what they call the highest, those that can be situated at the level of the central nervous system, to those that take place at the level of the guts and entrails and that, God knows why, they call inferior.

What matters, in other words, is calling into question this terracing of entities that tends to make us understand organic mechanisms in hierarchical terms whereas they are in fact perhaps to be situated at the level of a certain radical discord between perhaps three registers that I designate as Symbolic, Imaginary and Real. Even their reciprocal distances are not homogeneous. There is already something arbitrary about putting them on the same list. What does it matter, if these registers can at least have a certain efficacy when it comes to introducing the question?

Be that as it may, as soon as we are dealing with the level of a certain passion or suffering, as soon as we are dealing with thought – and there is nowhere that we can grasp the one who is thinking it as a consciousness – with thought that cannot grasp itself anywhere, a thought of which it can always be asked who is thinking it, that is enough to make anyone who enters into this strange dialectic renounce, at least for himself, the prevalence of thought insofar as it is something that grasps itself.

It means that the psychoanalysis must not only have read Freud to some extent, bearing in mind the psychological world's little boxes, which make it clear from the outset that 'you are you, and I am me', and, as for me, given that I am a psychoanalyst, I am of course the bright spark whose job it is to guide you around the labyrinth of a seraglio I have supposedly long been familiar with.

At the level of his practice, the psychoanalyst must always be able to present himself as the one who knows how much he is dependent upon things that, in theory, he fully grasped in his inaugural experience, and knows, for example, that he is dependent upon a certain fantasy. That is in theory certainly within his reach. He must not take the view that he knows on the grounds that it is in his capacity as what I call the subject supposed to know that they come to see him. They do not consult him about that which is marginal to some knowledge, be it that of the subject or common knowledge, but about that which eludes knowledge, and specifically about something that is precisely what every one of them definitely does not want to know.

Why would he not want to know if not because this not-knowing is what calls him into question as the subject of knowledge? This applies at the level of the simplest and, let's say, least informed being.

The analyst does not believe that he can introduce himself into such a question purely by accepting the role that has devolved upon him in the shape of the subject-supposed-to-know. He knows full well that he does not know, and that there is a danger that all he can construct as his own knowledge will be constituted as nothing more than a defence against his own truth.

Everything that he can construct about the psychology of the obsessional, everything he can embody in the so-called primitive tendency will not, when what is called the transferential relationship goes a little further, prevent him from being called into question in the fundamental mode of neurosis, to the extent that it involves the slippery interplay between demand and desire. Nothing in a case can be displaced if the psychoanalyst does not actually feel that it is his desire that interests the hysterical demand, that it is his desire that the obsessional wants to arouse at all cost.

But it is not enough for him to respond to that appeal by demonstrating to each of his questioners that we have here forms that have already been passed and reproduced in accordance with the law that regulates relations with everyone's relationship with their partner. It is not enough for him to move the question back to, I don't know what reiteration, which will always be retroactive. That is no doubt an essential dimension if the subject is to be made to understand that part of him he has dropped in the shape of an irreducible core. But without any scaffolding, all the many complicated constructs that are designed to explain the subject's resistances, defences and operation, this or that more or less desirable illness, cannot represent anything more than superstructures, in the sense of fictive constructs.

These constructs are designed solely to separate the analysis from where, ultimately, it is being tracked down. In other words, they come to represent – for the subject – what the progress of the analysis must make him renounce, namely the object, which is at once a privileged object and a scrap-object, to which he himself is bracketed. That is a tragic position because, ultimately, the analyst must know how to eliminate himself from this dialogue as something falls out of it, and falls out of it for ever.

The discipline that is incumbent upon him is therefore the opposite of the discipline incumbent upon a scientific authority. I do not say the discipline of the scientist [*savant*]. Modern science's scientist has indeed a singular relationship with his social surface and his own dignity, and it is far from the ideal form that is basically what constitutes his status. Everyone knows that what specifies the most contemporary forms of scientific research is by no means identifiable with the traditional type of scientific authority, with the authority of he who knows and touches, who operates and cures through the presence of his authority alone.

It is so pathetic to see the voracity with which some of those who understand what I have been teaching for so many years pounce upon my formulae in order to turn them into articlets [*articulets*] with only one thing in mind: taking credit for them, all that in order to take credit for having written an article that stands up. Nothing could be more different from what we should be helping them to find, namely the right situation of asceticism or what I would call 'destitution': that is the situation of the analyst to the extent that he is a man like any other, and one who must know that he is neither knowledge nor consciousness, but is dependent upon the desire of the Other, just as he is on the speech of the Other.

So long as there are no analysts who have understood me well enough to reach that point, nor will there be what that would immediately generate, namely the essential steps that we are still waiting for in analysis, and which, by retracing Freud's steps, would make it advance once more.

BIO-BIBLIOGRAPHICAL NOTES
by Jacques-Alain Miller

.

The first of these lectures was given in October 1967 at the Centre hospitalier du Vinatier in Lyon; the second in Bordeaux on 20 April 1967; and the third on 10 June 1967 at the Faculté de médecine, Strasbourg.

A stencilled transcript of the Lyon lecture was published by the CES de psychiatrie de Faculté de médecine, Lyon-I in 1981; it was republished, with my authorization, in the journal Essaim. Transcripts of the other two lectures were circulated.

The Asile du Vinatier, created by the law of 30 June 1838 that provided for a mental asylum in every département, suffered for a long time from its negative image and was known as 'l'Asile de Bron'. Reformed after the Liberation of France, it had already become the Centre hospitalier du Vinatier when Lacan visited it. The establishment is now the Rhône-Alpes region's main psychiatric centre.

The philosopher Henri Maldiney, who was born in 1912 and who taught at the Université de Lyon for a long time, had links with the phenomenological movement. His work concentrated mainly on poetry, the fine arts and Western and Chinese landscapes.

There was a large Lacanian group in Strasbourg. It developed from the mid-1950s onwards around Lucien Israel, a professor of psychiatry and a psychoanalyst. It was his idea to invite Lacan to Strasbourg.

Lacan visited Bordeaux at the invitation of a number of interns at the Hôpital psychiatrique (CHS) Charles-Perrens. The lecture took place in a municipal building opposite the establishment.

Printed in the United States
by Baker & Taylor Publisher Services